Our *Love Affair* with *Commercial Real Estate*

Our *Love Affair* with *Commercial Real Estate*

HOW TO BE SUCCESSFUL

Charles & Sherry Feitel

atmosphere press

Published by Atmosphere Press

Cover design by Ronaldo Alves

Atmospherepress.com

Table of Contents

Preface

"Real estate is not about property; it's about people."

– Barbara Corcoran

Welcome to your next big adventure: a career in real estate. This book is for the next generation of commercial real estate professionals who want to build a booming business.

What's a "booming business"? I'm glad you asked. From my perspective, it's building a business for life that you love. You might love building a booming business in commercial real estate because it helps others as we do in the medical and healthcare real estate business.

You might love it because it lets you make a lot of money if you're in the ranks of the top performers. But most of all, it allows you to wake up daily and manage your time how you want.

The freedom of being a top performer in commercial real estate fires me up. Regardless of what fires you up, if you're reading this book, you've likely just received your real estate license or are in the first few years of your new career.

On the other hand, if you are considering real estate as a new profession, I aim to share as much as I can to help you based on my experience building a booming business over the last three decades.

As you'll soon read, my start was rocky. But that's not unusual. Looking back, I don't regret anything. I found my way. I love my work. It gives me meaning that energizes me while making a difference for our employees and clients.

If you're ready to build lasting success and wealth in commercial real estate, you'll learn much about yourself. If you're as hungry to learn as I think you are, by the end of this book, you'll have the confidence and clarity to advance your career in real estate.

Acknowledgments

There's no way I could write this book without the help of my life partner, Sherry, and everyone in our firm who's contributed to our success. She is the one who inspired me at the beginning of my career. Today, we're best friends. We work in the business with other family members, and all the sacrifice, hard work, and dedication have paid off for us as they will for you.

I'd like to thank my parents and grandparents for teaching me the value of discipline, hard work, and a work ethic. My father wanted to be a doctor from the time he was a teenager. My grandfather sold the family car and took a bus to work in 1953 to afford my dad's medical school tuition. I have been lucky to have many positive role models in my life. We will learn about the power of choosing great role models later in the book.

Sherry and I have raised a great family, which is more important than any amount of money or success, in case you're wondering about our priorities.

Our family bond is love. We are utterly loyal to one another. We are each strong individuals in our own right. But it's the family values and always looking out for each other that keep us close together. That's the only way Sherry and our three adult children can work effectively together. In essence, we intentionally built a family-owned business.

Sherry is the glue of it all. She loves her kids unconditionally but still has high expectations for core values that matter. Her love for me and our marriage is a fierce, unbreakable bond. As a family, love, loyalty, and core values matter.

It's the values that keep us together. Our business is booming primarily because of who we are as people and as a team; our values and talents align well. You'll learn more about core values and team building later in the book.

If you're brimming with anticipation and perhaps a dash of uncertainty about what comes next in your career, I wrote this book for you. Congratulations are in order, but so is a dose of reality. Every year, millions of new real estate agents embark on this journey, lured by the promise of financial independence, the flexibility of working from home, and the allure of setting their hours.

However, success in real estate is not guaranteed. Success in any business requires hard work, dedication, and a strategic approach. As you'll see in the following pages, there's a process for building a booming business, and I will give you the template to write a strategic blueprint you can follow.

Success in any business is rare. The success rate for real estate agents can be challenging. According to industry statistics, about eighty-seven percent of all new real estate agents fail within the first five years of their careers.[1] The high failure rate is often due to ineffective marketing and insufficient training. But in the end, failure is about many things that are within your control and not. The key is for you always to do your best and keep learning.

On the bright side, current employment projections for real estate brokers and agents project three percent growth from 2022 to 2032, which is about average compared to

[1] https://blog.tomferry.com/87-of-all-agents-fail-in-real-e

other occupations.[2] Current projections indicate that while significant challenges exist, opportunities for success exist if you are well-prepared and persistent.

But don't get caught up in being average by focusing too much on industry averages and statistics. The bottom line is success is up to you. No matter the interest rates, the economy, or other factors, there is almost always a way to adapt your action plan and make a living in commercial real estate. It's up to you to live within your means while you build your business, make more money, save, and invest well.

More than anything else, consider this book your blueprint for success. It is part autobiography and part business book because, by design, there is a strong connection between my family and business life. I hope you find it relatively easy to build your business in a way that enhances your quality of life, whether you have a family or not.

Each chapter offers the insights and guidance needed to transform your commercial real estate dreams into reality. Remember, the value of any goal lies in the effort you invest in achieving it. Stick with it.

You have the right book if you're committed to being one of the top commercial real estate producers in your office and market. I will reveal everything I've learned while building my commercial real estate brokerage business over the last thirty years. I'll include relevant stories about my experiences and how essential my life partner, Sherry, and family have been to my success.

My hope for you as the reader is that you relate well to my story and use the tools I'm giving you as you see fit. I'll reveal the approach, mindset, strategic planning process, and toolkit that helped me and my family build our dream commercial real estate company. Apply what you need to your business,

[2] https://www.bls.gov/ooh/sales/real-estate-brokers-and-sales-agents.htm

and see what happens next.

Business is booming for us because we love our work. We chose a strong niche in medical offices and related properties, and we've been building our company since the mid-1980s.

I wish the same for you. Enjoy your journey.

Chapter 1

From Rookie to Rock Star

"Knowing yourself is the beginning of all wisdom."

— Aristotle

We all start as rookies. I know I did. But I've learned a few things about building a booming business in commercial real estate, and I'm thrilled you're with me for the journey.

If you're in the first few years of building your business, the first few chapters will provide you with the fundamentals for success. Even if you've been in the industry for years, focusing on the fundamentals is critical, and we'll get to that later.

Commercial real estate is like any other business. If you're determined to build a successful career, you're prepared to start with the fundamentals and practice what you have learned for decades.

Living life well is about knowing yourself well. Some of us learn who we are and what we want sooner than others and become determined to get it. I had no idea I would become a successful commercial real estate professional when I graduated from law school. I had to practice law long enough before realizing it wasn't for me.

Pro Tip: The more you know about yourself and what you want, the easier it is to see who you're not and what you don't want. That's powerful wisdom.

Be Hungry to Succeed

I needed to deliver pizza to make enough money to pay my bills until I got my real estate license. Getting my license was the easy part.

Chances are, you have your real estate license and you're working hard to figure out a way to make enough money to live the lifestyle you'd like. If you're hungry enough to buy, read, and apply the suggestions I give you, you dramatically increase your probability of success.

Everything I wrote in this book is from my direct experience. I've made many mistakes, but as you'll soon see, I don't see mistakes as failures. I've made a lot of money and continue to do so. And I love learning how to improve.

I'm not ready to retire, so you'll learn what my team and I are practicing today. We're expanding our business to metropolitan Phoenix, a booming market for our commercial real estate focus on medical and healthcare practitioners and their properties. I encourage you to notice the mindset I describe on the following pages so you can use it as your example.

Improve Yourself and Your Business

I know you're into self-improvement because you bought my book. Everything in it is about improving your commercial real estate business. Whether you're more of a lone wolf or part of an established real estate firm and team, expect practical insights, stories, steps, and strategies for being more successful.

When most of us are young, energetic, and full of confidence early in our careers, we typically don't have a solid career plan. In the case of commercial real estate, your career is a business if you look at it that way.

You are a living, breathing, thinking, acting, licensed real estate agent. Your focus is commercial. Expect to learn every day. Even though my book may give you a few good ideas on building your real estate business, practical experience is the best teacher.

I don't have all the answers. I'm not the biggest producer in the world. I don't have a way to help you beyond sharing what I've learned.

Before I walk you through a quick chapter overview, here's how a negative experience can turn positive, given your mindset. Being a heads-up rookie can make all the difference when we look for new opportunities.

Making a Career Change Into Commercial Real Estate

When I started the business in the mid-1980s, everyone wanted to be rich. As I write this book, I see that everyone wants to be rich. Wanting to be rich is the American Dream in many respects. Some things never change.

Making a career change into commercial real estate was a big move for me. I didn't know about being in real estate until I had enough experience working as an attorney to know that wasn't my career. The last thing anyone wants is to work in a career that doesn't let them realize their full potential. But wisdom comes with time and experience.

Being rich isn't only about money. As you'll see, it begins with your mindset. Wealth is a state of mind. A big part of being rich is enjoying your work. Before commercial real estate, I first worked as an attorney because when I was young, I thought I wanted to do that.

One of my early cases was a divorce and custody case. Our client was the husband, and he was the "model" husband in many ways. On the other hand, his wife was less than stellar, and there was plenty of evidence and pictures to prove it.

We spent months preparing for the case. On the day of the trial, I was well-prepared, confident, and excited about my case for the husband. Unfortunately, the judge saw things differently.

Before we even presented our side of the case, he ruled for the wife and awarded her custody of the children. The judge's long-time views of the family decided the case without any discussion.

Because of the experience, I no longer wanted to be a trial attorney. Working on that case changed my mind by waking me up to what I didn't want to do. Trust that your experience working in your chosen field will teach you about yourself.

Here's how I figured out I wanted to be in real estate. Way back after we first met, and before we fell madly in love and started working together, my best friend and life partner, Sherry, asked me, "Chuck, what do you want to be when you grow up?"

I knew I didn't want to be a lawyer at that point. I said, "I want to be a real estate developer." We were living in Memphis, Tennessee, at the time. Real estate was booming, and everything about it looked attractive to me. Real estate promises unlimited income potential and minimal structure compared to the legal profession.

It was as if the real estate industry was calling me by name, but Sherry pointed out that real estate developers need money. I was twenty-six, and I didn't have any money. But I knew what was next, and I was gung ho to go after the real estate business.

The biggest problem I faced when starting was making enough money to pay my bills. I started learning to lease apartments, fix toilets, and deal with tenants, but I knew that wasn't the way to become a wealthy real estate developer.

At first, the leasing aspects and interactions with clients were appealing. The money wasn't great, and the work was thankless. For example, dealing with maintenance issues isn't fun, but I learned a lot from my experience, which was invaluable.

Sherry eventually suggested that I become a broker so I could eventually earn enough money to develop properties. Sherry always gives me great advice. She's been with me the entire way, and I couldn't have achieved our firm's success without her.

But nobody starts as a broker until they get enough experience and decide they want the added responsibility.

I needed to find a way to make a lot of money. I was hungry to learn and grow. My journey through residential management was a stepping stone. But I soon realized I was creating wealth for others without reaping the rewards myself.

As a young, ambitious person, I craved more and was willing to take risks to achieve it.

Fortunately, I got hired by a fast-growing local real estate company. The firm represented developers and real estate companies. The fast-paced action of the people and transactions was alluring. The energy and pace were perfect for me. I was ambitious and shooting for the stars.

After about a year, Sherry joined me at the same firm. We worked together for three and a half years until we started our real estate brokerage. We founded our company, Health-Pro Realty Group, in January 1996, in Bethesda, Maryland.

We've been learning, growing, and creating family wealth ever since. Today, our adult children work in the business. They are the future of our brand.

What to Expect

Chapter 2 delves into the critical aspects of launching and sustaining a successful career in commercial real estate. Starting with the adage, "Do the best that you can until you know better, then when you know better, do better," the chapter emphasizes the importance of mastering fundamental practices in the field.

The real challenge lies in consistently applying and refining your skills.

Chapter 2 guides you through the initial career planning steps, stressing the need for a clear, strategic blueprint. You'll learn the value of patience, continuous learning, and a commitment to ethical practices.

We'll also cover the significance of passion and perseverance. Through personal anecdotes, we explain that maintaining strong client relationships and focusing on providing value can lead to lasting success. The chapter also explores how technological advancements reshape the industry, urging professionals to stay adaptable and resilient.

Finally, we'll review the importance of choosing the right firm and managing expectations. The emphasis is on playing the long game and building a sustainable, successful career in commercial real estate.

Chapter 3 is about "Street Smarts." It underscores the importance of gaining practical experience and learning from mistakes in the real estate business. Beginning with Oscar Wilde's quote, "Experience is the name everyone gives to their mistakes," the chapter emphasizes that many new agents make the error of jumping into client acquisition without a solid understanding of the business. Instead, the chapter advocates sticking to a well-thought-out plan and building trust and expertise.

Using Health-Pro Realty Group's model, Chapter 3 highlights the importance of professionalism and expertise, especially in specialized fields like medical real estate. Clients expect their real estate agents to be as knowledgeable and professional as their counterparts in law or medicine.

Anecdotes illustrate the high costs of ignorance and the crucial role of fiduciary duty in real estate transactions. It emphasizes that building a business with ethical and professional standards leads to long-term success and client trust.

The chapter also discusses the need for creativity and innovation in developing a business model. It highlights the importance of staying informed about market trends, such as the shift to remote work and online shopping, to help clients find value and save money.

Long-term planning and bold innovation are essential for sustained success.

Overall, Chapter 3 provides a comprehensive guide to building a successful and sustainable career in commercial real estate through experience, continuous learning, innovation, and a commitment to professional and ethical standards.

Chapter 4 is about marketing yourself. It emphasizes the power of focus and passion in advancing one's career, illustrated by Gary Keller's quote: "It is those who concentrate on but one thing at a time who advance in this world. Passion for something leads to disproportionate time practicing or working at it."

The chapter advises choosing the right firm, focusing on a specific niche, and building long-term relationships as critical strategies for success. It explains that the firm and you must cultivate your brand. It suggests defining your unique value proposition, constructing a compelling narrative, and consistently demonstrating the qualities and values you want to be known for. The chapter also emphasizes the importance of creating a cohesive visual identity, maintaining a consistent brand voice, and engaging in content marketing to establish yourself as an authority in your field.

Lastly, we'll cover the importance of ethics and integrity in all transactions, noting that these core values distinguish you in a competitive market and ensure sustained success.

Chapter 5 is about mastering sales and negotiation. It begins with a powerful quote by J. Paul Getty: "You must never try to make all the money that's in a deal. Let the other fellow make some money, too, because if you have a reputation for always making all the money, you won't have many deals."

This principle underscores the importance of fairness and mutual benefit in deal-making, which helps generate further opportunities. In the early stages of business development, canvassing new leads through phone calls, email, and social media is essential.

Building relationships based on mutual respect and trust is fundamental, and technology, while helpful, is simply an enhancement when used well. You'll learn the value of participating in online and offline activities to build these relationships, especially within your market niche.

The core of this chapter is my sales process, the Feitel Sales Process. It focuses on understanding client needs, educating them, facilitating transactions, encouraging them as needed, maintaining professionalism, and closing deals by empowering clients to make informed decisions.

Pro Tip: Authenticity and transparency are vital for long-term success, and trust and integrity are the cornerstones of the sales process.

The chapter concludes by emphasizing the importance of continuous learning and trying new things in sales. We'll cover public speaking and building relationships through vendor partnerships. Ethical behavior is paramount, and taking compensation only from your broker ensures a successful, long-term career. The art of closing deals is about serving clients as a trustworthy professional, ultimately leading to successful transactions and lasting relationships.

Chapter 6 is Excelling in Brokerage Services. We'll delve

into brokers' essential roles in commercial real estate, representing tenants and landlords. It begins by exploring tenant representation, highlighting how tenant reps assist clients in finding the perfect space and negotiating favorable lease terms. The chapter emphasizes the importance of thorough market analysis, strategic negotiations, and continuous support to prioritize clients' interests.

Additionally, the chapter introduces innovative solutions like shared listings, demonstrating how brokers can adapt to market changes, such as those caused by the COVID-19 pandemic. By emphasizing long-term relationships and continuous adaptation, Chapter 6 provides invaluable insights for anyone looking to excel in the competitive commercial real estate brokerage world.

Chapter 7 is Developing Expertise in Market Analysis. We will dive deep into the intricacies of mastering commercial real estate market analysis. Louis Glickman's wisdom, "The best investment on Earth is Earth," underscores the importance of understanding market dynamics for success in this field. This chapter emphasizes that thorough market and property analysis is crucial for any agent or broker aiming to excel.

The chapter begins with an overview of essential market analysis components, including economic indicators like GDP growth, employment rates, and interest rates, which significantly influence property values and demand. It also covers vacancy rates, rent growth, and emerging market trends such as sustainability and technological advancements.

Ultimately, this chapter equips agents with the knowledge and tools necessary to become market experts and provide exceptional value to their clients. By mastering market analysis, agents can anticipate changes, identify opportunities, and make informed decisions, ensuring long-term success in the competitive world of commercial real estate.

Chapter 8 is about the power of successful role models. By

modeling my mindset and business model after people and companies I admire, you will understand more about my personal experiences building a booming real estate business.

The chapter concludes by stressing the importance of taking personal responsibility, continuously seeking self-improvement, and surrounding oneself with people who challenge and inspire. Doing so can set the stage for a fulfilling and prosperous career in the real estate industry.

Chapter 9 delves into the art of building a great real estate team. Whether you become part of a team or build your own, the chapter emphasizes the importance of teamwork and strategic intelligence in achieving long-term success.

Real estate is fundamentally a people business. Successful transactions rely on professionals executing their roles effectively. The chapter highlights the importance of building and managing relationships with various stakeholders from brokers and lenders to lawyers and designers, ensuring smooth and efficient transactions.

The chapter also stresses the significance of shared values within a team. Trust, respect, and mutual support foster a collaborative environment, enhancing efficiency and project outcomes. Upholding ethical standards and continuous professional development are essential for maintaining a positive reputation and achieving long-term success.

Chapter 10 is about the power of teamwork. In this compelling chapter, we delve into the essence of what transforms individual excellence into collective success. We'll explore how the synergy of a well-coordinated team can elevate your real estate career.

The focus will be on building a robust network, fostering meaningful relationships, and investing in team dynamics. Discover how aligning with a strong team can boost your confidence, enhance your networking efforts, and ensure smoother transactions.

As we approach the book's final chapters, Chapter 11 is about learning to manage your real estate business in ways that complement the life you want. We'll explore how loving what you do is the key to great work.

We'll emphasize that passion drives effort, creativity, and success. To thrive in the commercial real estate business, align your goals with your passions, build a sustainable business model, and focus on financial management.

Developing a strong team and nurturing customer relationships are crucial. Embrace innovation, invest in personal development, and expand your network. Strategic planning will guide your business toward long-term success. Remember, your dedication and love for your work will ultimately lead you to greatness. The final chapter is where we pull all of your hard work together. I assure you that if you finish my book and apply what you learn to improve your business, starting immediately, you will be very pleased three, five, and ten years from now.

Your Path to Stardom

The journey from rookie to rock star is a continuous self-discovery, learning, and growth process. You can achieve greatness in your field by knowing yourself, setting SMART goals, developing a growth mindset, building a solid foundation, networking, embracing innovation, and cultivating resilience.

Remember, the path to stardom is not a straight line but a series of steps and missteps that lead to success. Stay committed, stay passionate, and let your journey unfold.

Now, let's focus on the fundamentals in Chapter 2.

Chapter 2

Commercial Real Estate Fundamentals

"Do the best that you can until you know better, then when you know better, do better."

– Maya Angelou

Regardless of where you are in your commercial real estate business, the fundamentals of building a successful business remain the same. Congratulations, and welcome to the game if you recently got your real estate license.

You now have a high understanding of the real estate business. But what you learned in real estate school was how to pass the test!

Passing the test is the easy part. Learning and practicing the fundamentals of commercial real estate brokerage, regardless of your niche or market, is the key to long-term and sustainable success.

Several residential firms have probably already approached you. But you want a career in commercial real estate. In this chapter, it's time to plan your launch with clarity, confidence, and success.

Are you considering launching your business in a big city or rural area? Do you know anyone in the field? It's daunting, so where do you start? The plan and/or blueprint should be your first mission, which means making fundamentally sound decisions from the beginning can help you get traction sooner.

Even if you've been in the business for a while and want to prosper, take a beginner's mindset and write a new strategic blueprint for you and your real estate business. Let's assume you answered the "why" question of commercial real estate with financial independence, autonomy, and wealth.

Now, we need to attach the "how" question. How will you learn the business? The "nuts and bolts." The fundamentals.

Mentors make a massive difference when you're willing to be coachable. You need a mentor. One of your first objectives is to find the right firm, team, or mentor for you. By the right mentor, I mean someone in the business who is successful, someone you admire and respect, and who is willing to guide you as you do the work.

Your Business Approach Is Fundamental

Building your business is a process, not an event. The methods, people, systems, and technologies you use in your industry are the foundation of all fundamentals. Given this mindset and approach, you're preparing to build your business for long-term success more than short-term gain and profit.

Nobody learned to build a successful commercial real estate business by reading a book, watching a video, or sitting through a weekend seminar. The best way to learn any business is to be in it and learn from successful people who have what you think you want for yourself.

Learning from an experienced professional who's figured out how to be successful for over thirty years can make a world of difference. A few people in my family and company wondered why I would want to tell the world how we've been successful. They were concerned that writing the book would give away "secrets" to competitors.

My first response is that nothing in this book is a "secret."

As I already mentioned, you can find real estate fundamentals in many places. As for helping the "competition," few people can consistently focus and act on what I'm revealing, even with the wisdom I share in my book.

Passion Is Fundamental

Sherry and I love the work we do. We don't have jobs. We are passionate about serving our clients and owning a thriving business that serves the needs of our clients. We've built an outstanding reputation over the years, doing the right thing for our clients.

> **Pro Tip: Being passionate about your life or business is a mindset. Imagine building a successful real estate business and loving the journey because you get meaning from helping people in your market.**

You need to have a legitimate passion for what you are doing. If you don't, take a close look at the path you're on and do some serious reflection. Relationships take a long time to build and a longer period to maintain. You must be willing to invest the most valuable thing, "time."

Sherry and I have had clients since I started in the business. If you take proper care of your clients and relationships, you will be a success. You may find what we have discovered: your clients are an extension of your family.

Be patient with yourself. There's no fast track to building a successful business. Fundamentals guide us. Find the fundamentals that guide you.

Sherry has preached for years that "patience" is critical. I always saw sales as somewhat sleazy, which I'll touch on later in the book. Sherry wisely convinced me that honest, patient, and sincere salespeople are the top performers in every business, with few exceptions.

Always put the client first. Always be honest, and you will go far in sales.

Your Mindset Matters

Expect change to be constant. While the commercial real estate industry has significantly evolved over the past thirty years, it remains fundamentally the same.

Substantial shifts in market dynamics, investment strategies, and operational practices have occurred, but real estate remains a relationship business. The advent and integration of technology will continue to propel change in the real estate industry.

Moreover, adopting innovative technologies such as artificial intelligence (AI), the Internet of Things (IoT), and blockchain has begun transforming the commercial real estate landscape, offering new opportunities for automation, enhanced security, and smarter buildings. These technologies contribute to more sustainable and efficient operations, better client service, and improved decision-making processes.

As the industry continues to evolve, the impact of technology on commercial real estate is undeniable. It has changed the industry's operations and influenced the fabric of commercial real estate investment and management, paving the way for future innovations and growth.

Regardless of industry changes, nothing is more important than your mindset. One key characteristic of your success is your commitment to focusing and being resilient. Resilient professionals take a long view of their business and career path.

The most successful people in commercial real estate and

other industries invested decades to master their trade. You'll never stop becoming a master if you're a master.

$600,000 Commission

Many years ago, I was able to make my first large deal. Here's a story about one of our first big commission checks. Early in my career, I wrote a paper giving a local hospital several development options, including fee ownership, condominium, and an equity model.

One day, a friend and client of a local hospital system called me with several questions about the hospital's ownership of a medical office building on campus. He asked me to write a "White Paper" that he could submit to his superiors. He was a young, bright VP climbing the hospital system corporate ladder.

After many gyrations, several consultants, and three years, the hospital hired a development partner and me to develop and lease the building. Two years later, we fully leased the building.

As a result, I received over $600,000 in leasing commissions. In addition, my friend and client is now president of a major health system and is at the top of his industry. It took time and patience, but we did it right, and it worked. That's an example of how doing the right thing and building relationships with the right people can pay off in the long run.

I have never refused a client because they were too small. When growing your business, refrain from focusing only on money and chasing big deals. My rule of thumb was always that if the deal was in healthcare, I would work it.

Sherry, my best friend, business partner, and life partner, always tells people that small deals become more significant deals later. Moreover, gaining another client will always return to you later in your career.

To support my case, Sherry saw an opportunity with the "baby boomer" doctors and dentists over a decade ago. Sherry gets all the credit for helping our firm become respected in the medical and healthcare space. She proposed we start selling healthcare practices.

We would attend trade shows in New York and Las Vegas and meet many older doctors, dentists, and optometrists nearing the end of their careers. My real estate broker license legally allows me to sell a business.

Always cautious, I was hesitant since I had never done it. Sherry confidently said, "With a law degree and twenty-plus years of experience brokering healthcare real estate deals, you have the skill and training to sell a business."

In most states, you do not need a license to sell a business. But you do need a license to sell real estate. Medical practice brokers who sell dental offices and medical practices often contract to sell or lease the real estate even though it's illegal.

The concept they purport to espouse is simple but needs to be revised. Here's a hypothetical example:

A dentist wants to sell a business worth $500,000. He wants to sell the office condo for $500,000. He wants to sell both for $1,000,000.

Let's say a buyer is only willing to pay $400,000 for the business. Many practice brokers will tell the dentist they will sell the real estate for $600,000, so the dentist will net $1,000,000.

Here are the flaws I see in the hypothetical example:

1. The real estate is worth the appraised value only. The practice broker may want to get $600,000, but if the bank says it's worth $500,000, he can only get $500,000. A licensed real estate broker would know this.

2. Next, the buyer and seller go under contract for the business for $400,000 and the condo for $600,000.
3. Next, both parties engage lawyers. After thirty days and $10,000 in legal bills, the bank appraisal comes in at $400,000. The seller wants $500,000, and the deal implodes.

None of this is likely to happen with a knowledgeable broker. Medical practice brokers charge eight percent in the Washington metro area to sell a business, but real estate brokers charge ix percent to sell real estate.

So, in my earlier scenario, the business and real estate would sell for $1,000,000, and the commission would be $80,000. If a practice broker sold the company for $500,000 and the real estate broker sold the condo for $500,000, the total fee would have been $70,000.

So, the business broker working without a real estate license costs the client $10,000 more and is not licensed to close the transaction.

Pro Tip: The moral of the story is stick to your chosen profession, and be the best professional fiduciary you can be for your clients. Avoid the temptation of greed.

The reality of our business is that we have sold many dental offices, which has led to the sale of many medical practices. That's because almost all medical or dental practices include real estate.

Choosing the Right Firm

Choosing the right real estate firm is one of the most critical decisions. You can also join an established team within that firm. Some firms and teams want you to have a college degree and a few years of experience. Shop around and choose what feels like the best fit if you're just starting.

Other commercial firms might recruit and hire rookies. It's up to you to do your homework and find a firm with a culture, compensation, and support structure that is suitable for you.

Regardless of where you start, the key is to manage your expectations. Be realistic about your goals and timelines. Know the resources your firm offers. Some large firms require a narrow level of focus.

Years ago, I interviewed a young guy at a competitive firm. He had been working on tenant rep deals for five to seven years. He was running into landlord opportunities through his contacts, but his firm would keep him from working those deals. Instead, he was required to refer those deals to the firm's landlord agents in return for a small referral fee.

He would have had to find another broker and firm if he had not been willing to accept how his firm managed him and their policies. You may find yourself in a similar situation more than once. That's why it's essential to contribute to your industry, especially in your local market.

Get involved in committees, nonprofit organizations, and civic groups as you gain experience and build relationships. New opportunities will present themselves as you focus on contributing to your community, industry, and firm.

The better you know yourself, the easier it is to choose a firm and culture that works well for you. Find a firm that supports you if you're incredibly independent and self-disciplined. If you need lots of structure, support, and the accountability of a team or manager, take that approach.

Also, don't be worried about your commission split at the beginning of your career. Your firm may offer you eighty-five percent of the fee, but if you need to learn how to execute, eighty-five percent of zero is still zero!

You need to learn how to generate leads, take a deal from A to Z, and be a professional. Later, if you think the split is unfair, you can always work elsewhere. Someone will appreciate your ability. Agents jump around a lot for pennies. Focus on the dollars. Agents often jump from firm to firm, looking for a few more dollars in a split, a sign-on bonus, or a more impressive title. Some people fall for that, and others don't.

Play the long game. Grow every year and get better and better in your field. It's a three-to-five-year learning curve with no shortcuts. My team grows significantly every year because of the entrepreneurial environment we have created. In the iconic movie *Wall Street*[3] from the eighties, Gordon Gekko said, "Give me guys young, smart, and hungry, and I'll make them rich."

Your real estate career is a long-term game. Once Michael Jordan became **Michael Jordan**, his success didn't depend on who he played for. His success was because of his raw talent and work ethic. Jordan practiced and worked harder than practically anyone else in the sport. That's what led to his legendary success.

I need to emphasize the commitment to a long-term play. Get-rich-quick schemes have been out there since the beginning of time. Commercial real estate brokerage is a relationship business. It takes time to build solid, genuine business relationships.

Moreover, every real estate deal has a "story" behind it. The more deals you make, the more stories you have. Stories take time to develop and unfold. Don't rush the story.

Do it right, do it honestly, and the story will unfold.

[3] https://en.wikipedia.org/wiki/Wall_Street_(1987_film)

Commercial Real Estate Fundamentals

The commercial real estate (CRE) market is a dynamic and multifaceted sector that plays a crucial role in the global economy. It encompasses nonresidential properties used for business purposes, including offices, retail spaces, industrial units, and more. Economic conditions, interest rates, and supply and demand dynamics significantly influence CRE, making the market sensitive to broader economic trends.

Commercial real estate operates through expansion, recession, recovery, and boom cycles. Recognizing and adapting to these cycles is essential for successful investment and strategic planning.

The lingering effects of global events, such as the COVID-19 pandemic, have heightened the market's complexity, introducing new challenges and opportunities. For instance, shifts toward remote work have impacted demand for office spaces, while e-commerce growth has increased demand for industrial and warehouse properties.

Investors and professionals in the CRE market must navigate these complexities with agility and informed decision-making. To assess property values and investment potential accurately, becoming a top producer involves understanding key market indicators, such as vacancy, rental, and cap rates.

Embracing the complexities of commercial real estate with a keen eye on market trends and economic indicators can pave the way for a rewarding and successful career in this sector. As professionals embark on their CRE journey, maintaining flexibility and a commitment to continuous learning will be vital in navigating the market's inevitable shifts and capitalizing on the opportunities they present.

Commercial Property Types

The earlier you can find your niche or focus in real estate, the better. It's up to you to learn as much as possible about your market and your interests and choose the best professional direction. Some of us take longer than others to get traction. It's natural that over your career, you may pivot from office to something more specialized like industrial or medical. You'll learn as you go.

Virtually all commercial real estate (CRE) professionals focus on specific property types, each offering unique investment opportunities and challenges. Real estate professionals, investors, and institutions should be familiar with these segments to navigate the market effectively.

Here's a high-level overview of the key property types:

1. **Office Space:** This category includes buildings used for office purposes, ranging from skyscrapers in city centers to small office buildings in suburban areas. Office spaces are further classified into Class A, B, or C, reflecting their quality, location, and amenities.

2. **Industrial:** Industrial properties are for manufacturing, production, distribution, and storage. They can include heavy manufacturing, light assembly, bulk warehouses, and flex industrial spaces.

3. **Retail:** Retail properties house businesses that sell goods and services directly to consumers. This segment includes shopping centers, malls, retail storefronts, and mixed-use buildings that combine retail with other uses.

4. **Multifamily:** This sector comprises residential real estate designed for multiple families, such

as apartment complexes, high-rise condominium buildings, and multifamily housing units.

5. **Hotels:** Hotels and hospitality properties cater to travelers and include full-service hotels, limited-service hotels, boutique hotels, and resorts.
6. **Special Purpose:** Special purpose properties are designed for a specific use and don't easily fall into the other categories. Examples include churches, schools, and government buildings.
7. **Mixed-Use:** Mixed-use developments combine several property types into one project, such as retail, office, and residential spaces coexisting in a single building or complex.
8. **Land:** Land investment involves undeveloped property. Investors purchase land to develop it for commercial use or sell it at a profit when its value increases.

Property types have unique market dynamics, including demand drivers, investment strategies, and risk profiles. A deep understanding of these segments allows real estate professionals and investors to make informed decisions, tailor their strategies to specific market conditions, and mitigate risks associated with market volatility.

Key Terminology and Concepts

Understanding critical real estate concepts and terminology is crucial for anyone involved in the commercial real estate (CRE) sector. This knowledge prevents misunderstandings from derailing deals and enhances one's ability to communicate effectively with clients, negotiate deals, and make informed decisions.

Here are some essential terms every CRE professional should know:

- **Gross Rental Income (GRI):** The total income deducted from all leases before any expenses.
- **Vacancy Factor:** The percentage of all available units or spaces unoccupied and not generating income.
- **Effective Gross Rental Income (EGI):** Gross rental income minus vacancy and credit losses accurately reflects a property's income.
- **Total Operating Expenses (OpEx):** All costs associated with running and maintaining a property, excluding mortgage payments or financing costs.
- **Net Operating Income (NOI):** A property's income after subtracting operating expenses from the Effective Gross Income. NOI does not include taxes and financing expenses.
- **Common Area Maintenance (CAM) Fees:** Fees are charged to tenants to cover the costs associated with the upkeep of common areas within a property.
- **Capitalization Rate (Cap Rate):** The Cap Rate is the NOI divided by the property's current market value or purchase price.

Take Your Fiduciary Role Seriously

My overall suggestion in this regard is that if you take a listing, do your very best on behalf of the seller. Don't get greedy with fees. Work hard on behalf of your client, and the money will come. Likewise, the same applies if you are the tenant's agent. Take your fiduciary duty seriously and work on behalf of your client. Never put your interests before a client's.

Don't attempt to take other people's business away from them. If it's your listing, others should not act as if it is theirs. You can't go wrong with honesty, integrity, and professionalism.

As the dust settles on these sweeping changes, it becomes clear that the real estate landscape is on the brink of a significant transformation. The implications of the new regulations are profound and far-reaching, particularly for the average homebuyer and seller.

With commissions falling directly on buyers' shoulders, the industry must adapt and innovate urgently. One potential outcome of this shift is a heightened demand for transparency and fairness in real estate transactions.

Now more than ever, buyers will seek value for their money and demand that their agents act in their best interest without hidden fees or conflicting loyalties. The recent changes could lead to more independent and buyer-focused real estate firms prioritizing their clients' needs over corporate profit margins.

Moreover, the change may encourage technological advancements that simplify the home-buying process, making it more accessible and less costly. Online platforms could emerge, offering competitive alternatives to traditional brokerage services, reducing buyers' overall cost burden, and increasing market efficiency.

The new reality necessitates a reassessment of sellers' selling strategies. With buyers shouldering more financial responsibility, sellers may need to price their homes more competitively to attract prospective buyers who are now more cost-conscious. New rules could lead to a more balanced market in which we price properties more in line with their actual market value, benefiting buyers and sellers in the long run.

However, these changes are not all positive. The burden of additional costs on buyers may exacerbate the affordability crisis, particularly in high-demand urban areas. Policymakers and industry stakeholders must work together to address these challenges, perhaps through subsidies or financing options that make professional representation more accessible to a broader range of buyers.

In conclusion, while the residential real estate market changes present significant challenges, they also offer growth and improvement opportunities. By embracing transparency, innovation, and fairness, the industry can navigate this paradigm shift and emerge stronger, ensuring that all parties involved in real estate transactions are better protected and served.

What matters the most for you is committing to ethical practices and client-focused service, which are your highest priorities as you grow your real estate business.

It's also important to know that when you put the principles of my book to work for you and your team, you'll be prepared to prosper no matter what the real estate industry, interest rates, or politicians do.

Chapter 3

CRE Street Smarts

"Experience is the name everyone gives to their mistakes."

– Oscar Wilde

Learning the intricacies of the real estate business is crucial. Many people get their licenses and immediately start cold-calling for clients—a huge mistake.

Always stick to your plan and cultivate your blueprint for success. People will work with you if they trust you as their advisor. If you don't know the business, why would they work with you? Real estate is a professional field like law, medicine, and accounting.

Mastering the Fundamentals

First, you need to learn the jargon and real estate terms. Everyone wants to jump to the deal stage, but slow down.

Know the fundamental terms and how they apply in various situations. As a trusted professional, you must know what you do for your client. We'll cover more on that shortly.

Professionalism and Expertise

Take a look at Health-Pro Realty Group's model. On the tenant rep side, our clients are doctors, dentists, optometrists, and veterinarians. They spend many years in school to learn their trade. After a residency honing their skills, the state requires them to earn a license to practice. They expect the same level of professionalism from their real estate broker.

Our knowledge and expertise are why they choose to work with us. Think of it this way: if you need an operation, you want a doctor with experience and the ability to help you.

Our clients have the exact requirements when choosing a real estate agent. Take fiduciary duty seriously and improve your skills to give your client the best representation possible.

Understanding Key Concepts

Years ago, I was listing a commercial office building. A residential agent with no commercial knowledge called me with a prospect. The first question was, "How much is the rent?" Fair question. I responded, "Twenty dollars gross." Gross includes all expenses in the rent.

So, if the space is 2,500 square feet, the rent is $50,000 per year or $4,166 monthly. The inexperienced agent thought gross meant net, so she thought the tenant would have to pay $20 per square foot plus building expenses.

Back then, a building cost $10 per square foot, so she thought the annual rent was $75,000 or $6,250 monthly. Medical leases are often ten years, so that misunderstanding could have cost their client $250,000 over the lease term.

The High Cost of Ignorance

Not knowing what we don't know and being a fiduciary in commercial real estate can cost clients a lot of frustration and money. Ignorance can also cost the inexperienced agent their license if the mistakes are costly enough.

Real estate transactions have many facets, including market TIA dollars, market free rent, market annual escalation, and lease terms, just to name several of the most extensive domains of expertise in learning your market and serving clients.

Not long ago, I needed laser corrective surgery. I found my surgeon through three simple criteria: how many procedures they had performed, years of experience, and reviews from other patients.

Pro Tip: When you build experience and confidence, you become a professional your clients can trust. Trust is everything.

When seeking an agent to ensure the best representation, your clients will ask similar questions. Learn as much as you can about your niche. Subject matter expertise is crucial in setting yourself apart from the competition.

Fiduciary Duty and Professionalism

Know what you are doing before you jump into the deep end as a trusted commercial real estate advisor. Imagine a client suing an inexperienced agent and broker for costing them a quarter of a million dollars simply because they didn't know what they didn't know, such as the difference between net and gross rent.

Moreover, here is another simple mistake agents make all the time. Most gross leases have a clause saying the tenant is responsible for yearly increases in real estate taxes and operating expenses.

In my thirty-plus years of experience, thirty percent of commercial agents do not advise their clients of this concept because they simply don't understand it. If the annual increase kept pace with the most recent CPI index of three percent per year, that could amount to thousands of dollars on the lease.

The bottom line is you have a fiduciary responsibility to advise and serve your clients. It's up to you to take your education seriously. Surrounding yourself with successful role models in your market is also crucial.

Serving Your Client's Best Interests

I emphasize the importance of building your business with the highest possible ethical and professional standards over time. I often see agents compromising their clients' needs to satisfy their own.

Regarding your fiduciary obligations, it's illegal to act in your self-interest. Clients are trusting you to serve their best interests. If you do it right, the money will come.

The Need For Continuous Learning

No book I know of teaches these essential points of real estate. Do your research, uncover a mentor, settle in for the long haul, and learn the business from the ground up.

If you understand the basics, you will only add value to your clients as you gain experience. You have to earn your experience by being consistent with your marketing and networking efforts, which will accelerate your learning while making a living by closing deals.

Life is short, and when you look back, you want to be

known as a successful agent or broker who helped people succeed in their businesses while being respected as an expert in your field!

Creativity and Innovation

You must become a student of your market, the economy, and people because dealing with people is the most crucial skill set you can develop.

Being a student of the market helps you be more informed than many of your competitors. For example, when writing this book, I was aware that millions of tenants now work from home and will not return to the office soon. The world has dramatically changed how we work since the pandemic locked us down for too long. That's one of the reasons owners and managers of commercial office space are having significant challenges.

The owners of office buildings who can't cover their expenses, including debt service to their lenders, end up losing their properties to the banks. Because of that, thousands of lenders will sell nonperforming assets to real estate investors.

The point is that staying informed will help you help your clients find value and save money. For example, if you knew you could acquire free rent or buy an older office building and convert it to medical use, you could improve the property, fill it up with new tenants at market rents, and make a lot of money serving your clients.

Another macroeconomic trend affecting commercial real estate is the shift from retail shopping to online shopping or e-commerce. Retail shopping is way down, and billions of dollars that used to go to these stores are gone. The money moved online.

You can't live well in commercial real estate by selling online property. You create a booming business by being a constant and continual learner, networker, and professional dedicated to advising your clients.

Exploring Alternative Uses

Let's tackle office space first. Is there an alternative use for traditional office space? The growing trend of adaptive reuse is offering several innovative solutions:

1. **Residential Conversion:** One of the most popular alternatives is converting empty office buildings into residential units. This approach can help address housing shortages in urban areas. While this may alleviate the housing crisis, there are more complete solutions. Factors such as zoning laws, building codes, and the financial viability of such projects must be carefully considered.
2. **Hotel Conversion:** Another viable option is transforming office spaces into hotels. Hotel conversions are especially relevant in areas with high tourism or business travel demand. However, developers must navigate challenges such as structural modifications and obtaining necessary permits.
3. **Alternative Asset Classes:** Beyond residential and hotel conversions, office spaces are being repurposed for other uses, such as life science labs, industrial spaces, or coworking environments. Depending on the location and market demand, these alternatives might be more financially viable. For instance, life science conversions have become

increasingly popular due to the rising demand for research and development facilities.

4. **Educational Facilities:** Another alternative is converting office spaces into classrooms or educational facilities. Educational facilities can benefit cities with a growing student population or where educational infrastructure needs expansion.
5. **Flexible Workspaces:** The shift toward remote work and hybrid models has increased the demand for flexible workspaces. Converting traditional office spaces into coworking spaces or flexible office setups can cater to the needs of start-ups, freelancers, and remote workers.

As an agent, it is crucial to research the viability of these alternative uses and make informed recommendations to your clients. Understanding market trends, zoning regulations, and financial implications will help identify the best possible uses for vacant office spaces. Additionally, ensuring that all traditional marketing methods are exhausted, such as spec suites, more extensive concessions, and bonus commissions, can enhance the attractiveness of these properties.

Be the Last Agent Standing

Remember that the creative agent is the last one to get fired. Years ago, a senior broker explained that agency leasing was analogous to the children's game Musical Chairs.

In this game, you run around a circle of chairs as the music plays. When the music stops, everyone scrambles to find a seat. If the chairs are gone, you lose the game. The last kid sitting, or the last one with a chair, wins the game. This analogy perfectly captures the competitive nature of real estate.

> **Pro Tip: Be curious. The source of creativity is curiosity. If you're curious by nature, you'll be drawn to learn more about your market and how to best serve your clients by delivering consistently high value.**

In the commercial real estate market, the principle remains the same. Each property listing represents a chair, and the brokers are the players. As the market demand grows, there will be fewer options. The broker who continues to market creatively and persistently will ultimately be the one who secures the final deal. Just as in Musical Chairs, it's about endurance, strategy, and timing. The last broker standing with the listing will make the commission.

Moreover, this analogy also emphasizes the importance of adaptability. In the game, players must quickly adapt to changing conditions, much like brokers must adapt to market trends and client needs.

Staying ahead requires creativity, a keen awareness of the market landscape, and an ability to pivot strategies when necessary. The most successful agents can navigate these changes smoothly, ensuring they remain in the game until the end.

A Story of Innovation

Many years ago, a Yale University student wrote a term paper proposing a revolutionary idea for shipping logistics. His idea was to centralize the shipping of mail and products across the United States.

For example, if you were shipping a letter from Arizona

to California, it would first go to a central hub in Memphis, Tennessee. From there, employees would sort it and send it overnight to its final destination in California.

Great idea, right? Not in the professor's mind. The professor gave the student a D, deeming the idea impractical and unrealistic.

That student was Fred Smith, and despite the initial skepticism, he founded Federal Express, now known as FedEx. Smith launched the company in 1971 with a clear vision to revolutionize the logistics industry by prioritizing time-sensitive shipments.[4]

That was on April 17, 1973. Federal Express began operations in Memphis with a fleet of fourteen aircraft, delivering 186 packages to twenty-five cities across the United States on its first night. The innovative hub-and-spoke system allowed for efficient sorting and overnight delivery, which became the cornerstone of FedEx's success.

Today, FedEx is a global giant valued at $66 billion, known for its continuous commitment to innovation and efficiency in the logistics and transportation sectors.[5] The company can attribute its growth and success to Smith's visionary idea and relentless pursuit of excellence despite early doubts and challenges.

This story illustrates the power of innovation and perseverance. It reminds us that even the most groundbreaking ideas may initially face skepticism, but with determination and strategic execution, they can transform industries and create lasting impact.

---

[4] https://www.fedex.com/en-us/about/history.html

[5] https://medium.com/@imabd489/from-a-c-grade-at-yale-to-founding-fedex-the-inspiring-journey-of-frederick-smith-5299c5068230

Specializing in Your Niche

If you haven't found a way to specialize in a niche you are passionate about, I encourage you to find a way to differentiate yourself as a specialist. My company, Health-Pro Realty Group, only leases and sells medical office space.

Fortunately, medical properties are in high demand even with the commercial downturn. Most doctors cannot perform medical and dental procedures over a computer, so they need clinicians and office space.

While technology continues to evolve and bring innovative solutions to the healthcare industry, the fundamental need for physical space remains. Every doctor, dentist, and optometrist requires "sticks and bricks" to practice effectively.

At first, we worked with healthcare professionals but were generalists, handling office, retail, and industrial clients. This broad approach allowed us to gain many experiences, but it also diluted our expertise.

Many more prominent household names, such as Cushman, CBRE, and JLL, have a medical division, recognizing the value of specialization in this niche market. However, for our small firm, specializing in medical office real estate has enabled us to hone our skills and provide unparalleled service to our clients.

My mother often used an old saying: "Jack of all trades, master of none." This saying has profound implications in real estate. By focusing exclusively on medical office spaces, we have become true masters of our trade. We understand medical professionals' unique needs and challenges, from compliance with health regulations to integrating advanced medical technologies.

The demand for specialized knowledge in the medical real estate market is significant, considering the size and scale of medical and healthcare practices in America. Investors are increasingly attracted to medical office buildings due to their stability and the essential nature of healthcare services.

For instance, technological updates in the office and exam room can significantly enhance the patient experience and improve operational efficiency. As we navigated this niche, we discovered that deep expertise allows us to offer tailored solutions that generalists might overlook.

From the optimal layout for a dental clinic to the specific infrastructure needs of an ophthalmology practice, our specialization means we provide real value to our clients, ensuring their facilities meet all requirements and enhance patient care.

Long-Term Planning

Again, take the time and have a long-range plan of attack. Don't be afraid to do something outside the realm of normality. Taking a chance and rolling the dice is vital to being a differentiator and trendsetter. Long-term planning is more than just a road map; it's a strategic framework that aligns your daily actions with your ultimate vision. It allows you to anticipate trends and prepare for challenges, ensuring your business remains resilient and adaptable.

A well-crafted long-term plan outlines your goals and provides a detailed strategy. Planning involves examining interactions between various investment proposals and available financing choices, exploring different options, and developing contingency plans to avoid surprises. By considering multiple scenarios, you can make informed decisions that balance risk and reward, positioning your business for sustained growth while doing the same for your clients.

Moreover, long-term planning encourages innovation. When you have a clear vision of where you want to go, you're more likely to experiment with new ideas and approaches that differentiate you from the competition. This willingness to step outside your comfort zone can lead to groundbreaking solutions and opportunities. As the famous saying goes, "Fortune favors the bold." Embracing this mindset can transform your business into a trendsetter in your industry.

However, it's important to remember that long-term planning is not a one-time event but an ongoing process. Regularly revisiting and adjusting your plan ensures it remains relevant and aligned with your evolving business environment. Developing an action plan can help turn your long-term vision into reality by increasing efficiency and accountability within your organization. This proactive approach will help you stay ahead of the curve and capitalize on emerging opportunities.

Managing Business Risk

I'll repeat this throughout the book: Don't fear failure. Failure is a crucial part of success when you learn from your mistakes. Many real estate billionaires have faced bankruptcy at some point.

Embrace failure as a learning experience to transform setbacks into stepping stones. Analyze what went wrong, adjust your strategies, and move forward with newfound wisdom.

> **Pro Tip: Failure is not the opposite of success but a part of it. Navigating these challenges builds resilience and fortifies your path to success.**

Change is a constant in any business. The market, technology, and consumer preferences are constantly evolving. Stay informed about these changes to anticipate shifts and adapt your strategies accordingly. This proactive approach helps you stay ahead of the curve and maintain a competitive edge.

Learning the fundamentals of your business type is crucial. This foundational knowledge provides the bedrock for your expertise. However, expertise alone is not enough. To stay cutting edge, you need to be the subject matter expert in your field.

Understand the basics and master the intricacies of your industry. Engage in ongoing education, attend industry conferences, and network with professionals. Doing so positions yourself as a leader and innovator in your field.

Risk management involves practical steps such as prioritizing risks, buying insurance, and limiting liability. Implement a quality assurance program to ensure your products or services meet the highest standards, reducing the likelihood of failure. Limiting high-risk customers and maintaining a diverse client base can mitigate potential losses.

Chapter 4

How to Market Yourself

> *"It is those who concentrate on but one thing at a time who advance in this world. Passion for something leads to disproportionate time practicing or working at it."*
>
> *– Gary Keller, founder of Keller Williams*

Position Yourself Like a Pro

People want to work with good people they can trust, especially regarding real estate transactions involving large amounts of money and documentation.

If you take the time to give back, it shows your commitment to your fellow person. That may sound corny, but it's repeatedly proven true.

In the early 2000s, our son attended a private middle school in suburban Maryland. The school was interested in acquiring the building next door. I volunteered to facilitate the transaction since the school needed CRE experience.

It took a lot of time, and the fee would have been six figures, but the satisfaction I enjoyed in closing the deal was fantastic. Children and parents achieved their goal of growing the school, and I was the broker who made it happen.

Also, a few years earlier, I served on a foundation board that raised significant funds to build a new pediatric ER. The ribbon-cutting ceremony was extra special because Sherry and I had helped raise money for such a considerable community project.

Pick a charity near and dear to your heart and get involved. You don't need to overthink this. For kids and animals, there is no correct answer. If you are helping people in need, it is worthwhile.

Try to serve where you can be significant. I wanted to help the local Children's Hospital early in my career. Sick children need help, and back in the 1970s, my father was the hospital president, which made it even more significant for me. However, the board was full of billionaires and celebrities from big cities like Washington, DC. I learned to invest my time elsewhere, and so will you.

So, I served on a few smaller community hospital boards and was able to be more of a "big fish in a small pond." You will better feel where to give your time and money as you get more involved and mature.

> **Pro Tip: Everything but the fundamentals of building professional relationships, managing employees, and being top performers has changed since Sherry and I started Health-Pro Realty Group in the late 1980s.**

Back then, we utilized the "power of the pen" by writing articles on healthcare real estate. Today, sharing your expertise through articles, podcasts, speaking engagements, and social media is fundamentally the same but much more accessible.

It doesn't cost much to position and promote yourself in many cases. Here are key fundamentals to consider:

1. **Choose Your Firm Wisely:** Starting at an established firm is typical for beginners. You don't need your name on the brokerage firm to be successful and happy. Being part of a great team can make a significant difference. Collaboration and shared

knowledge within a firm can significantly boost your expertise and success.

2. **Focus Is Power:** Focus on one thing and become the expert in your market. The volume of deals you close correlates directly with your earnings, making town size a significant factor. Remember, you will sometimes change your focus based on your tenacity and ability to adapt.
3. **Build Long-Term Relationships:** Focus on building and maintaining relationships to grow a solid pipeline of deals. Not all deals will close, which is a reality of the real estate business. With experience, you'll better navigate these challenges by taking a collaborative and team approach.

Building Your Brand

The firm you work with has a brand. So do you. So, let's define what brand means in terms of your brokerage firm and you.

Pro Tip: A brand is the unique identity of a product, service, or business that distinguishes it from others in the market.

Brand encompasses everything people think when they hear the brand name, including its perceived quality, value, and image. A brand has established visual elements like logos, color schemes, and typography, as well as the overall customer experience and reputation maintained by leadership, managers, and employees.

Essentially, a brand is how a product or business is perceived by those who experience it, including customers, employees, and the media. It is an easily recognizable identity that communicates the product or service's values and promises.

You are your product and the service positioned as a commercial real estate professional. It's up to you to know yourself well and stick with the fundamentals of branding.

You don't need to be a marketing wizard to establish and maintain a strong brand. Here is a list of things to consider when branding yourself and ensuring your business is booming.

1. **Define Your Purpose and Unique Value Proposition:** Clarify what makes you unique and how you add value to your clients. Create a concise statement that describes who you "help" or serve.
2. **Audit Your Brand Equity:** Evaluate your current personal brand and how it is perceived among your peers and clients. Reviews or audits will help you understand your starting point and areas for improvement.
3. **Construct Your Narrative:** Develop a compelling story that aligns with your firm's mission and values. This narrative should convey your professional journey, expertise, and passion.
4. **Embody Your Brand:** Consistently demonstrate the qualities and values you want to be known for. Your behavior, appearance, and communications should all reflect your brand.
5. **Create an Appealing Visual Identity:** Design a professional look with a logo, color scheme, and typography consistent with your firm's branding. Ensure your visual elements are cohesive across all platforms.

6. **Use a Consistent Brand Voice:** Maintain a consistent tone and style in your communications. Whether through social media, emails, or presentations, your voice should reflect your brand's personality and values.
7. **Engage in Content Marketing:** Share valuable content that showcases your expertise regularly. Content marketing can include articles, blog posts, videos, and social media updates relevant to your industry and audience.
8. **Network and Build Relationships:** Actively engage with your professional community online and offline. Attend industry events, join professional groups, and participate in discussions to build and maintain relationships.
9. **Monitor and Adapt:** Review feedback and performance metrics regularly to understand the impact of your branding efforts. Be prepared to adjust to stay relevant and aligned with your personal and firm goals.
10. **Align with Your Firm's Brand:** Ensure your brand complements and enhances your brokerage firm brand. Your values, messaging, and visual identity should harmonize with the broader organizational brand to present a unified image to clients and stakeholders.

Core Values Matter

Live your life with integrity. Your character, not your wealth, defines your legacy. People remember core values, including authenticity, compassion, integrity, courage, respect, honesty, creativity, innovation, leadership, loyalty, responsibility, self-discipline, teamwork, trustworthiness, wisdom, empathy, and gratitude.

Consider the legacy of a high-profile billionaire known for his wealth but remembered for his poor treatment of people. Money is just one aspect of success. Reflect on your daily actions and strive to be honest, helpful, and empathetic.

At Health-Pro Realty Group, professionalism is critical. Our most minor deal was three hundred square feet, and our largest was several hundred thousand. Regardless of size, we pride ourselves on our expertise in the healthcare field.

Values should guide every decision you make. They create a strong foundation for long-term success and reputation. Building a business on solid ethical grounds ensures financial success, meaningful relationships, and a lasting legacy.

Key Platforms, Applications, and Tools

Commercial real estate professionals today have access to a wide range of technology platforms, applications, and tools.

> **Pro Tip: Choosing the appropriate tools for your firm and type of business is critical. It's also essential to get the input of everyone on your team who must also learn and use the technologies you choose.**

Naturally, your broker will have platforms and tools they want you to use, and it's up to you to stay committed and use them like everyone on the team expects and agrees. Here's a high-level overview of top-performing firms and agents' most shared tools.

1. **CRM Software:** Customer Relationship Management (CRM) software is crucial for managing client relationships, tracking interactions, and ensuring follow-ups. Popular options include Salesforce, HubSpot, and AscendixRE, among many others.
2. **Multiple Listing Service (MLS) and Commercial Information Exchange (CIE):** Access to comprehensive listing databases like MLS and CIE is essential for finding properties, comparing market trends, and analyzing data. These platforms provide detailed information that helps you stay competitive.
3. **AI Marketing Tools:** Utilize AI-powered tools for targeted marketing campaigns. These tools help you analyze market trends, predict customer behavior, and tailor your marketing efforts. AI tools like ChatGPT for drafting marketing content and CRM integrations can significantly enhance your outreach.
4. **Lease Management Software:** Software like Lease Accelerator and Visual Lease streamlines the process of managing leases and rental agreements, ensuring compliance and optimizing lease administration.
5. **Professional Website:** A professional website can be your best online marketing asset if you invest in designing, writing, and maintaining it by trusted professionals. Ensure it is SEO-optimized, user-friendly, and regularly updated with new content. Integrate features like property search functions, client testimonials, and contact forms to engage visitors effectively.

6. **Social Media Platforms:** Leverage platforms like LinkedIn, Facebook, Instagram, and X to promote your brand, share market insights, and connect with potential clients. Consistent, engaging content helps build your online presence and establishes you as an authority in the field.
7. **Listing & Productivity Apps:** Apps such as LoopNet and CoStar offer comprehensive property listings and market data. Productivity apps like Trello and Asana help manage tasks and projects efficiently, keeping you organized and focused.

Connecting in Your Community

I've already shared how I got involved in our community and remain so today. The great news is you can choose how to connect with your community.

As a local real estate professional, your community involvement is crucial. Over the years, I've served on hospital and school boards. Giving back to the community, whether through time or money, is essential. It enhances your satisfaction and success.

People prefer to work with givers, not takers. Giving back shows your commitment.

We've touched on this before, but it's important to emphasize choosing a charity that resonates with you and getting involved. Your talents can significantly impact smaller, local organizations. Community involvement enhances personal fulfillment and strengthens your network and business relationships.

Supporting local initiatives and contributing to the well-being of your community demonstrates your investment in its future. It builds a positive image and fosters trust among community members, which can translate into business opportunities.

Personal Brand, Ethics, and Integrity

The US Army's tagline, "Be all you can be," applies to commercial real estate. Know your business, serve your clients, and uphold your fiduciary duty. Your clients will form their opinions based on their experiences and your reputation.

We have established ourselves as healthcare real estate experts in the Washington metropolitan area. Specializing in one area has helped us build a strong brand. You can't be an expert in everything. Focus on your niche and excel in it.

Maintaining high ethical standards in all transactions is crucial. Clients value trustworthiness and integrity. Your reputation as an ethical professional will precede you, making it easier to build long-term relationships and secure repeat business.

Ethics and integrity should be at the core of your brand. They distinguish you in a competitive market and ensure sustained success.

In closing, you are positioning yourself as a commercial real estate professional. Doing so demands a focused, strategic approach. Choose your firm wisely, concentrate on one area in which to become an expert, and build long-term relationships.

Your brand, both personal and aligned with your firm, is critical. Define your unique value proposition, maintain a consistent brand voice, and engage in content marketing. Utilize technology and tools effectively, from CRM software to social media platforms.

Always live by your core values. Integrity, empathy, and professionalism will define your legacy and build trust.

Community involvement not only enhances your fulfillment but also strengthens your network. Ethics and integrity distinguish you in this field, ensuring lasting success.

Chapter 5

Mastering Sales and Negotiation

"You must never try to make all the money that's in a deal. Let the other fellow make some money too because if you have a reputation for always making all the money, you won't have many deals."

—J. Paul Getty

Every deal helps generate two more deals. In the beginning, you will be canvassing new leads. Several of the most prominent methods are phone calls, email reachouts, and social media reachouts using Facebook, LinkedIn, Twitter, and Instagram. You also want to network and build relationships in your community.

Business development is a team and contact sport. You have to be involved in your community based on where you are in your career and life. Starting, you may not become the chairman of local nonprofit boards or the Chamber of Commerce. But you can commit yourself daily to the warm and cold prospecting that accelerates the growth of relationships and new business opportunities.

The bottom line is you need to create a system that works for you to manage your efforts accurately. One of the most overlooked disciplines in business development is following up with prospects and centers of influence at the right time.

Your network will include top-tier relationships like your

coworkers, broker, and current and past clients. Anyone who can refer a deal to you is considered a center of influence. Often, these are accountants, attorneys, business owners in your community, and relationships with people who like and trust you as a professional.

Building Relationships Is Fundamental

Nothing is more important than building relationships based on mutual respect and trust. You don't need technology to build relationships, but it sure helps. The building aspect of relationships includes participating in online and offline activities that expose you to people ideal for your business.

Suppose you follow my firm's example in the medical and healthcare space. In that case, you'll want to build relationships in your geographic market with people in the medical field, including doctors, medical complex owners and developers, and all related professionals willing to network with you.

> **Pro Tip: Your network can easily be translated to the value of your business. When you learn to network authentically and enjoy work for the purpose of building new relationships and trust, you will prosper.**

By networking online and offline, you'll build new relationships. As you build relationships, you'll want to record notes, key dates, related contacts, insights, and anything helpful in following up with people in your growing network.

I highly recommend Dale Carnegie's book *How to Win Friends and Influence People* if you've never read it. Carnegie wrote the book in 1936, selling over thirty million copies worldwide. It offers timeless advice on improving interpersonal skills and becoming more personally and professionally influential.

Before we touch on the fundamental importance of technology for managing relationships, here are several highlights from Dale Carnegie's classic book.

1. **Learn Fundamental Techniques in Handling People:** Show genuine interest in others, avoid criticism, and give honest appreciation.
2. **Six Ways to Make People Like You:** Become genuinely interested in others, smile, remember people's names, be a good listener, talk about the other person's interests, and make the other person feel important.
3. **Win People to Your Way of Thinking:** Avoid arguments, respect others' opinions, admit your mistakes quickly, and begin in a friendly way.
4. **Be a Leader:** Praise improvements, give the other person a fine reputation to live up to, and use encouragement.

Carnegie emphasizes the importance of understanding human nature and employing empathy in interactions to build stronger relationships and influence others effectively.

Managing Relationships – The Art of Following Up

One of the biggest mistakes I see salespeople and other professionals make is failing to follow up with prospects, clients, and strategic partners. Effective follow-up is crucial for maintaining and growing your business relationships. It demonstrates reliability, builds trust, and keeps you top-of-mind with your contacts.

However, managing all these follow-ups requires time and effort. Following up is where a good Customer Relationship

Management (CRM) system becomes indispensable.

Follow-ups are not just polite gestures but strategic actions that can significantly impact your business. A timely follow-up can differentiate between closing a deal and losing a prospect to a competitor.

> **Pro Tip: One of the most costly mistakes you can make is failing to follow up with people in your network whom you may serve and who also add value to your overall mission in your community.**

Consistent follow-ups show your clients you are dedicated, attentive, and professional. They help nurture relationships, turn prospects into clients, and turn clients into repeat customers.

I've already covered the importance of choosing and using the best tools for your business. One of the most critical tools for following up is your customer relationship management system.

Yes, using a system requires commitment and discipline. In the end, professionals who lack the discipline to follow up are less likely to succeed.

Here are some key benefits to consider for following up using the system of your choice:

1. **Appointment and Meeting Management:** A CRM can schedule and remind you of appointments and meetings, helping you manage your time effectively and ensuring you get all the essential engagement.
2. **Note-Keeping:** Take detailed notes on each interaction with your contacts. Notes will help you personalize your follow-ups and demonstrate that you remember and value previous conversations.

3. **Tracking Key Prospects:** A CRM allows you to categorize and prioritize your prospects based on criteria such as interest level, potential value, and stage in the sales cycle. You must focus your efforts where they are most likely to yield results.

4. **Managing Business Relationships:** Use CRM to maintain an up-to-date record of your business relationships, including those of strategic partners and clients.

5. **Automating Daily Tasks:** Automate routine tasks such as sending follow-up emails, scheduling calls, and updating contact information.

In the fast-paced world of commercial real estate, follow-ups can make or break your business relationships. Leveraging a CRM system ensures you stay on top of your appointments, meetings, notes, key prospects, and any business relationships you value.

It's a Small World

The world is smaller than most of us think. How you see the world determines how you engage with others, network, and build relationships that help everyone prosper.

If you've never heard of the phrase "six degrees of separation," here's what it means so you can apply it to your approach to business and life.

- The idea of "six degrees of separation" suggests that any two people on earth can connect by a chain of no more than six acquaintances.

- Psychologist Stanley Milgram first explored this concept in the 1960s through an experiment called the "small-world problem."
- Milgram's research found that a short chain of around six connections can link us together.[6]

Despite its vast size, this theory shows how closely connected our social world is. For instance, social media platforms make it easy to see these connections as we can identify mutual friends and acquaintances who bridge gaps between people from different parts of the world.

My experience with the six degrees of separation is that someone from the past contacts me out of the blue and wants to do business with me. In most cases, they remembered a past encounter we had.

The lesson is that you never know when a random act of kindness and doing the right thing, given the circumstances, will lead to a new relationship and business deal years later.

Negotiate With Power

I enjoy negotiating deals. Everyone has a unique style, and this is important. Years ago, I worked with a guy named John who was a great negotiator. He leased a small building in Rockville, Maryland, often showing space to smaller "mom-and-pop" prospects.

The market rate was $24 per square foot gross. After touring the space, prospects would ask John for the rate, which he would say was $24. If they wanted to negotiate, he'd say $28. The negotiation worked like a charm, making him one of the best landlord agents of his time.

[6] https://hbr.org/2003/02/the-science-behind-six-degrees

Pro Tip: The key to negotiating is confidence. You must know your market better than most of your competition. You must practice to improve your negotiating skills.

I have clients who excel at negotiating salaries or drug prices but need help with commercial real estate. There's a misconception that negotiating always means getting a lower price. It's about achieving a market deal.

If the market rent is $24 per square foot, negotiating down to $22 per foot might cost you elsewhere in the deal. A deal has many components: rate, tenant improvement allowance, and free rent concessions. As a tenant rep, work hard to get the best market terms for your client. As a landlord rep, provide sound advice based on market terms.

For example, many doctors think they are skilled negotiators. If the landlord says the rent is $28 per square foot and the doctor negotiates it down to $26, they might feel victorious. But if the market rate is $22, they overpaid. Knowing the market is crucial in effective negotiation.

Lawyers love to negotiate leases, charging $500 or more per hour. The problem is they know laws and contracts better than the real estate market. Clients often pay them a lot for "better deals," but they lack market insights.

Brokers sometimes ask for a year of free rent in markets where landlords aren't offering it. A lack of knowledge can make everyone suffer.

It's great to be firm and play "hardball," but you must know your stuff. Most commercial real estate landlords are wealthy and skilled. A fair deal benefits everyone involved. When both parties are happy, it's a successful negotiation.

Do business right, and you stay in business!

The Feitel Sales Process

My process, which we encourage our team of agents and brokers to use, has evolved over the years. We encourage everyone to be authentic, which means "not fake." I've mentioned that core values, integrity, and trust are musts.

Selling is helping my clients manage one of the most significant assets, which is often their office space and place of doing business. My sales process is what drives results. If you don't have a reliable process, you can't expect consistently better results.

Pro Tip: Selling is helping your clients get what they want. The best salespeople ask intelligent questions, listen, and serve their clients well.

Here's a breakdown of my sales approach so you can model yours after it:

1. **Understand the Need:** The first step is thoroughly understanding the client's needs. Understanding requires active listening and asking the right questions to uncover their goals, preferences, and pain points. Whether finding the perfect location for a new office or negotiating lease terms, we aim to align our services with the client's specific requirements.
2. **Educate Your Client:** Education is a critical component of the process. Clients often come with varying levels of knowledge about the real estate market. It's our job to provide them with all the necessary information to make informed decisions. Education includes market trends, property evaluations, and potential investment returns.

Being transparent and informative builds trust and positions us as industry experts.

3. **Facilitate the Transaction:** Facilitating the transaction means managing all the details to ensure a smooth process. Facilitating involves coordinating with various parties, including property owners, legal advisors, and financial institutions. Our role is to streamline communication and handle logistics so our clients can focus on their core business activities. Efficiency and meticulous attention to detail are paramount here.
4. **Encourage as Needed:** Negotiation is both an art and a science. Sometimes, clients need a little push to move forward, especially when hesitant or indecisive. Encouraging doesn't mean being pushy; it's about reassuring and highlighting the benefits of taking the next step. It requires a delicate balance of assertiveness and empathy to guide clients through potential reservations.
5. **Always Be Professional:** Professionalism underpins every interaction. Professionals are punctual, prepared, and respectful. It also involves adhering to ethical standards and maintaining a polished demeanor. Our clients rely on us to be the experts, and professionalism reinforces their confidence in our abilities.
6. **Close by Asking What the Client Would Like to Do Next:** The closing stage is about sealing the deal without pressure. After presenting all options and facilitating thorough discussions, we ask the client what they want to do next. We empower them to make the final decision, knowing they

have all the support and information they need. It's a respectful and client-centered way to conclude the transaction.

7. **Incorporating Authenticity and Transparency:** Authenticity and transparency are vital for long-term success. We encourage our team to be genuine when working with clients. We want everyone to show their true selves rather than adopting a sales persona. Authenticity fosters deeper connections and builds lasting relationships with clients. Transparency involves being honest about potential drawbacks and setting realistic expectations. Clients appreciate honesty and are more likely to return for future business.
8. **Building Trust and Integrity:** Trust and integrity are the cornerstones of our sales process. We operate with the highest ethical standards, ensuring every decision and recommendation is in the client's best interest. This approach enhances our reputation and creates a loyal client base that values our commitment to their success.

In conclusion, the Feitel Sales Process is client-centric, focusing on understanding, educating, facilitating, negotiating, and closing with professionalism and authenticity. By adhering to these principles, you can help your clients manage one of their most significant assets—their real estate—with confidence and trust.

To us, selling is not about closing a deal but building enduring relationships based on mutual respect and shared goals.

Becoming Your Best Self

Sales is a team and contact sport played at the game's highest levels. If you intend to build a booming commercial real estate practice, you've got to embrace selling and promoting yourself, even if it feels uncomfortable at first.

For example, everyone fears public speaking and looking like a complete idiot. But those of us who can overcome that fear do so by focusing on the audience and the value of our message.

In building your real estate business, consider selling as helping people get what they want. Your style and strengths will dictate your best prospecting strategies.

One of my agents loves face-to-face prospecting. He is on his game when knocking on doors and talking to future clients. He comes from a drug sales background and is very comfortable knocking on doors and visiting doctors and dentists in person.

Conversely, I used to have a guy who loved LinkedIn. Unfortunately, he lived and died by it and didn't make it. He put 100 percent of his efforts into LinkedIn, but LinkedIn alone doesn't always bring success.

However, the key is building relationships in your community instead of hiding behind social media platforms and other technologies. Diversity in lead generation will lead to more business and make you a better agent/broker.

I prefer a more diverse marketing campaign. As you grow and gain experience, try various approaches and systems. Focus on what works best for you, and occasionally push yourself out of your comfort zone.

If you consistently focus on improving your sales, networking, communication, and follow-up skills, you will be surprised by the results. Always be learning and trying new things.

Sometimes, your preferred method of canvassing gets stale, so it's good to rely on more than one strategy. As you become a subject matter expert, talks and lectures can also yield fruit.

Over the years, Sherry and I have specialized in the Washington, DC, Virginia, and Maryland markets. I have also lectured about our business in other states, such as New York, New Jersey, Pennsylvania, Illinois, California, and Nevada.

Public speaking has allowed us to share our vast experiences and learn how the business is similar to and different from our market. We also build relationships through solid vendor partnerships. Lenders, lawyers, builders, accountants, consultants, and others work closely with our client base.

Being Ethical

The love of money causes vendors to work with less-qualified people. Being unethical is a slippery slope that no one should go down. Work on behalf of your client and be professional in the level of service you provide. Ignore the temptation to make a quick buck in an illegal and immoral game.

Pro Tip: Only take compensation from your broker if you want to sleep well at night and build a successful, long-term career.

Remember, you have a fiduciary duty to represent your client. If you refer a bank, general contractor, or anyone else who pays for the lead, you act in your best interest, not the client's.

If a vendor partner wants to buy you dinner or take you to a ballgame, that's a nice gesture and promotes working together. If they offer money, say no. There are also CRE brokers who pay vendors for leads. Same story. NO.

Only pay fees to licensed agents and brokers. Only accept money from licensed agents and brokers. I'm passionate about this.

Most of my competition plays this game. The love of money is evil and doesn't work out well in the long run. Sherry always says we will be the last man standing. Do business the right way and honor your commitments to the profession.

You can make plenty of money legitimately.

The Art of the Close

One of my favorite movies is *Cadillac Man*, starring Robin Williams. At one point, Williams's character exclaims, "I love to sell."

If you love to sell like I do, you'll be successful by sticking to your authentic style of managing and building relationships. The art of the close is about doing your best to serve your client as a professional people can trust. That's your most important job as a fiduciary.

In summary, know your market, understand your client's needs, embrace educating and consulting clients, and do your best to facilitate smooth real estate transactions. Be your authentic, professional best every day. Choose to be skilled, and you'll close lots of deals.

Chapter 6

Excelling in Brokerage Services

> *"We are what we repeatedly do. Excellence, then, is not an act, but a habit."*
>
> *– Aristotle*

A broker typically represents the tenant or the landlord in commercial real estate brokerage. While the landlord usually pays the broker's fees or commissions, the beauty of this business lies in its negotiable nature.

Nothing is ever set in stone, making each deal unique and engaging. This chapter aims to help you excel in brokerage services.

Tenant Representation

Let's begin with tenant representation by discussing a typical lease scenario. A tenant representative, or tenant rep, assists the tenant in finding a suitable space, considering factors such as size, price, and, most importantly, location.

The tenant rep plays a crucial role in meeting the tenant's needs and preferences while navigating the complexities of the commercial real estate market. Here's an overview of the tenant representation positioning, process, and role.

The Lease Process

The lease process typically begins with the landlord issuing a lease proposal. This proposal outlines the terms and conditions under which the landlord is willing to lease the property.

The tenant rep then reviews this proposal and counters based on current market conditions. This negotiation phase is critical as it sets the foundation for the lease agreement. The tenant rep uses their expertise to ensure that the terms are favorable and competitive.

Landlords might ask tenants to submit their initial terms and conditions in some markets. While this approach can be beneficial in setting clear expectations, I prefer when landlords start the process.

This method provides a negotiation baseline and helps find common ground more efficiently. It lets the tenant rep better understand the landlord's priorities and constraints.

The Role of the Tenant Rep

The tenant rep's role extends beyond merely finding a space. They are responsible for conducting a thorough market analysis to inform the tenant about current market conditions.

The analysis includes rental and vacancy rates and any incentives landlords offer. With this information, the tenant can make an informed decision and leverage their position during negotiations.

Furthermore, tenant reps assist with financial analysis and comparison of various occupancy scenarios. The comparison ensures that the tenant understands the long-term financial implications of each option.

Whether it's a lease renewal or relocation, the tenant rep's goal is to secure the most favorable terms for the tenant.[7]

---

[7] https://www.modern-cre.com/insights/what-is-a-tenant-representation-broker-what-do-they-do

Negotiation and Beyond

Negotiations can proceed once there's a counter to the initial lease proposal. This phase involves back-and-forth discussions to refine the terms. Tenant reps use their market expertise to negotiate favorable terms and conditions, including rental rates, lease duration, tenant improvement allowances, and other concessions.[8]

After reaching an agreement, the tenant rep continues to provide support. This support includes overseeing the lease-signing process, ensuring that all necessary documents are in order, and ensuring that both parties fully understand the lease terms.[9]

The tenant rep may also assist in coordinating the move-in process and completing any tenant improvements to the tenant's satisfaction. Giving more like this is an excellent example of how you can model your differentiation and market reputation by going the extra mile for your tenants.

Long-Term Relationship

The relationship between a tenant and their rep does not end with the lease signing. A good tenant rep maintains an ongoing relationship with their client, monitoring market conditions and advising on lease renewals and expansions. They help tenants navigate any issues during the lease term and ensure that their clients are always in a favorable position.

Tenant representation is a comprehensive service beyond finding a suitable space. It involves detailed market analysis, strategic negotiations, and continuous support to prioritize

---

[8] https://www.astreetpartners.com/post/tenant-representation-services

[9] https://www.rentecdirect.com/blog/lease-signing-process/

the tenant's interests. A skilled tenant rep is an invaluable asset in the complex world of commercial real estate.

Brokering Deals

Understanding the broker's role is crucial. A broker arranges transactions between buyers and sellers. Once there's a meeting of the minds, it's OK to stop brokering.

Pro Tip: Over-negotiation can be counterproductive.

When both parties are aligned, it's time to finalize the deal. Again, the more experience you have in negotiations and transactions, the easier it will be for you to communicate your value.

Once the parties agree on terms, a lease is issued. Typically, tenants engage a lawyer to review the lease and all related documents. It's essential to remember that lawyers handle the legal terms, not the business terms.

They may need to be more familiar with market-specific rents and concessions.

Pro Tip: Let the lawyer handle the legalities and the broker handle the negotiations. The design and construction phase begins post-signing, which can take three months to a year.

A skilled broker can also assist tenants in procuring lease renewals. If a tenant wishes to stay, they need a new lease once the current one expires. Usually, leases max out at ten years.

Negotiating renewals well before the lease ends is critical to maintaining leverage. A proactive approach ensures better terms for the tenant, including rent and concessions.

Purchasing Property

The approach is similar when a tenant opts to buy instead of lease. However, purchasing property involves a sales contract rather than a lease, and the process often takes longer due to feasibility periods and various contingencies.

The feasibility period is a negotiated timeframe that allows the buyer to terminate the contract for any reason, ensuring that they have sufficient time to conduct due diligence.[10]

During this period, the buyer will thoroughly inspect the property, review financial documents, verify zoning and land use regulations, and ensure that the property meets all its requirements.

These requirements can include environmental assessments, structural inspections, and market analyses to confirm that the investment aligns with their business goals. If any issues arise, the buyer can either renegotiate the terms or withdraw from the deal altogether.

Commercial real estate (CRE) sales can take years, especially when dealing with large, complex properties or portfolios. The timeline is extended further by the need for financing, which involves securing loans and meeting lender requirements.

Also, be aware that various contingencies, such as the need for tenant leases to be in place or the completion of specific improvements, can prolong the process.

Clients often want to handle the purchasing process themselves, believing it will save time or prevent upsetting the current landlord. However, going it alone can be disastrous if one is inexperienced in purchasing commercial real estate. Costly delays are only one example of how acquisitions go wrong.

Real estate, banking, and financial professionals operate

---

[10] https://www.austintenantadvisors.com/blog/what-is-the-feasibility-period-when-buying-commercial-real-estate/

on established practices, and brokers are integral to that system. A seasoned broker provides invaluable expertise, ensuring that clients navigate the complexities of the transaction efficiently and effectively. They bring a deep understanding of the market, negotiation skills, and the ability to foresee potential pitfalls.

For instance, brokers can advise on leaseback options, where the seller becomes a tenant, providing immediate rental income for the buyer and ensuring a smooth transition.[11] They can also help structure deals to include favorable terms, such as extended closing periods or phased payments, which can be critical in large transactions.

In conclusion, purchasing commercial property is a multifaceted process that requires careful planning and expertise. Brokers are pivotal in managing this complexity, guiding clients through each step to secure favorable outcomes.

Your involvement is beneficial and often essential in ensuring the transaction's success.

The Value of a Broker

A common fallacy is that using a broker costs tenants money. Clients often believe that they ultimately pay commissions and that self-representation saves money.

In my experience, the brokers who provide the most market knowledge and the best communication and negotiation skills typically save their clients precious time, money, and legal exposure.

Consider a building in suburban Maryland that is leasing for $35 per square foot gross. The tenant pays $35 per square foot, and the landlord covers operating expenses and real estate taxes.

---

[11] https://www.robertdmitchell.com/sale-leaseback-commercial-real-estate

The landlord won't lease for less if $35 is the market rent. You also need to consider commissions and tenant improvement dollars (TIA) in this scenario. The market determines the concessions, such as free rent and TIA.

A skilled broker understands these market dynamics and can negotiate effectively on behalf of the tenant. For instance, I once negotiated a deal for an oral surgeon, saving him $500,000 in rent reductions and concessions without any cost. The landlord paid my firm $80,000, securing a tenant for another ten years.

That's a lot of value. Seek to provide value to your clients, and the money will follow.

Shared Listings and Creative Solutions

In response to the significant vacancies caused by the COVID-19 pandemic, I developed a creative concept of shared listings. Although many office buildings have reduced demand, healthcare-related businesses still need space.

We partnered with office brokers to place medical, dental, vet, and optometry practices in these buildings, benefiting landlords and brokers. It's a recent example of how knowing our market and being innovative enough to adapt can make a huge difference.

This arrangement requires cooperation but has successfully matched tenants with appropriate spaces. Adapting and innovating are vital in navigating market downturns and unforeseen circumstances like COVID-19.

The adage "When given lemons, make lemonade" aptly applies here. Continuously experimenting with new marketing and prospecting techniques keeps the business dynamic and forward-moving.

Roger Staubach, a Pioneer

Historically, brokers worked primarily with sellers and landlords, with buyers and tenants relying on the seller's agent. Football Hall of Famer Roger Staubach[12] revolutionized this by advocating for tenant representation and persuading landlords to compensate tenant reps.

Staubach's success led to the widespread adoption of tenant representation in commercial brokerage firms. That was his way of differentiating himself from anyone else.

Understanding who you represent is crucial. Landlord and tenant representation require different skill sets and allegiances. Breaching fiduciary duty can lead to legal consequences. Good brokers strive to make fair deals for all parties and find a middle ground.

As a landlord rep, you aim to achieve the highest rent or sales price with minimal concessions. As a tenant rep, you desire to secure the lowest rent with the most concessions. Good brokers know the market well and use their knowledge to negotiate favorable terms.

A Case Study in Market Realities

In 1986, a mentor told me that real estate is a perishable commodity, comparing vacant space to a banana. Fresh initially, it eventually goes bad if not used by a specific time. It's an interesting perspective.

I once represented a dentist whose landlord insisted on $45 per square foot for renewal despite market rates being in the high $20s to low $30s. We moved to a nearby space at $28 per square foot with better terms, and the original space

[12] https://en.wikipedia.org/wiki/Roger_Staubach

remained vacant for seven and a half years, costing the landlord nearly $800,000.

This story underscores the importance of realistic expectations and market knowledge. Successful brokerage is about creating value for all parties involved. It requires professionalism, honesty, transparency, and in-depth market knowledge.

Pro Tip: By understanding the nuances of landlord and tenant representation, brokers can effectively negotiate deals that benefit everyone. There's only one of you; your unique skills and insights are your competitive advantage.

In summary, we explored the intricacies of brokerage services in commercial real estate. We discussed brokers' roles and responsibilities in representing tenants and landlords, the importance of understanding market conditions, and the value brokers bring to the negotiation table.

Through real-life examples and case studies, we highlighted how skilled brokers can save clients money and secure favorable deals. We also introduced innovative solutions like shared listings to adapt to market changes.

Ultimately, excelling in brokerage services requires a blend of market knowledge, negotiation skills, and the ability to create win-win situations for all parties involved.

Chapter 7

Developing Expertise in Market Analysis

"The best investment on Earth is Earth."

– Louis Glickman

As I have said, market and property analysis are massive to becoming a successful agent or broker. Developing your expertise in your market means you have to know what information to stay on top of to serve your clients best.

This chapter overviews commercial real estate market analysis and highlights some of today's most common resources. One significant first step is learning about all the resources your broker offers.

Market analysis is crucial for any commercial real estate (CRE) agent. Understanding the market dynamics allows agents to make informed decisions, provide accurate advice to clients, and strategically position themselves in the industry.

Market analysis in commercial real estate involves evaluating various factors that affect property values, demand, and investment opportunities. These factors include economic indicators, vacancy rates, rent growth, and market trends.

Practical market analysis helps agents anticipate market changes and identify lucrative opportunities for their clients.

Critical Components Of Market Analysis

Conducting a thorough market analysis is essential for understanding the dynamics of a particular market and making informed business decisions. This section outlines the critical components of market analysis, providing a foundation for assessing market conditions, competition, and opportunities.

1. **Economic Indicators**
    - **GDP Growth:** A strong economy usually leads to higher demand for commercial properties.
    - **Employment Rates:** Higher employment can increase demand for office and retail spaces.
    - **Interest Rates:** These affect the cost of borrowing and can influence investment decisions. Rising interest rates may lead to higher capitalization rates and lower property values.[13]
2. **Vacancy Rates**
    - **Office Sector:** As high as it's ever been (as of 2025) because of COVID-19 driving people home.
    - **Retail and Industrial Sectors:** These sectors often exhibit different vacancy rates based on consumer spending and industrial activity.[14]
3. **Rent Growth**
    - **Multifamily and Retail Properties:** These segments have shown resilience with consistent rent growth, even amidst economic uncertainties.[15]

---

[13] https://www.jpmorgan.com/insights/real-estate/commercial-real-estate/commercial-real-estate-trends

[14] https://www.nar.realtor/commercial-real-estate-market-insights/may-2024-commercial-real-estate-market-insights

[15] https://www.jpmorgan.com/insights/real-estate/commercial-real-estate/commercial-real-estate-trends

- **Impact of Inflation:** Inflationary pressures can lead to higher operating costs and rents, affecting tenants' ability to afford space.

4. **Market Trends**
    - **Sustainability:** There is a growing focus on sustainable building practices and energy efficiency, which can enhance property values and attract environmentally conscious tenants.
    - **Technological Advancements:** Technology integration in property management and tenant services is becoming increasingly important.[16]

Conducting Market Analysis

1. **Data Collection**
    - **Primary Data:** Primary data includes direct observations, surveys, and interviews with industry experts and stakeholders.
    - **Secondary Data:** Reports from industry associations, government publications, and market research firms provide valuable insights.
2. **Comparative Market Analysis (CMA)**
    - A CMA involves comparing similar properties that have recently sold or are currently on the market to estimate a property's value. This method is beneficial for pricing and investment decisions.
3. **Site Analysis**
    - Evaluate the physical characteristics of a property and its surroundings. Consider factors

[16] https://www.dealpath.com/blog/commercial-real-estate-trends/

such as accessibility, infrastructure, and neighborhood demographics.

Common Resources for Market Analysis

1. **National Association of Realtors (NAR):** NAR provides comprehensive reports and insights into various aspects of the commercial real estate market, including vacancy rates, rent growth, and market trends.[17]
2. **JPMorganChase:** Their reports offer detailed analysis and forecasts on commercial real estate trends, focusing on economic indicators, market performance, and investment strategies.[18]
3. **Deloitte:** Deloitte's commercial real estate outlook provides insights into industry trends, risk mitigation strategies, and the impact of sustainability initiatives.[19]
4. **Dealpath:** Dealpath offers updates on market optimism, rental growth, and technological advancements in commercial real estate.[20]
5. **Reuters:** Reuters provides articles and analysis on economic trends, interest rates, and their impact on the commercial real estate market.[21]

[17] https://www.nar.realtor/commercial-real-estate-market-insights/may-2024-commercial-real-estate-market-insights

[18] https://www.jpmorgan.com/insights/real-estate/commercial-real-estate/commercial-real-estate-trends

[19] https://www.deloitte.com/us/en/insights/industry/financial-services/commercial-real-estate-outlook.html

[20] https://www.dealpath.com/blog/commercial-real-estate-trends/

[21] https://www.reuters.com/practical-law-the-journal/transactional/commercial-real-estate-trends-predictions-2024-2024-03-01

Practical Applications

1. **Staying Informed:** Review industry reports and market analyses regularly to stay updated on the latest trends and economic conditions. Subscribe to newsletters and attend industry conferences and webinars.
2. **Networking:** Build relationships with other industry professionals, including brokers, developers, and financial analysts. Networking can provide valuable insights and opportunities.
3. **Client Advisory:** Use market analysis to provide clients with data-driven advice. Help them understand market conditions, pricing strategies, and investment opportunities.

Mastering commercial real estate market analysis is essential for new agents. It involves understanding economic indicators, vacancy rates, rent growth, and market trends.

Utilizing resources such as NAR, JPMorganChase, Deloitte, Dealpath, and Reuters can provide valuable insights and support effective decision-making. By staying informed and leveraging these tools, agents can better serve their clients and succeed in the dynamic world of commercial real estate.

Specifically, we can access Costar, Loopnet, and CREXI in CRE. These sophisticated multimedia-based software programs offer tons of information, including asking rents, comps, available space, and absorption, just to name a few facts at the fingertips of any broker.

In addition to the media options, a good broker keeps a mental record of what is going on in the market. Good brokers also routinely talk and meet with their competitors to learn what is happening. They work together to achieve the client's goals and "make deals."

Flawed Logic

One of my competitors was leasing vacant space in Prince George's County, Maryland. They sent out a report claiming a demand for far more physical therapy groups in the county, attempting to argue why these groups should come to a specific property.

The flawed logic here lies in the assumption that there's a quantifiable demand for physical therapy groups in a specific part of the county. There is no reliable way to know such a fact without concrete data. It is essential to focus on the facts at hand and base decisions on factual data, not on subjective or speculative information.

> **Pro Tip: The best way to avoid flawed logic is to know your market thoroughly. That means becoming a dedicated student.**

You must understand key aspects of the commercial real estate market. Here are the critical elements to consider:

- **Market Rent in a Market:** Knowing the current market rent rates is crucial for setting competitive prices and negotiating leases. You must understand the average cost per square foot for comparable properties.
- **Market TIA (Tenant Improvement Allowance) in a Market:** Tenant Improvement Allowance refers to the amount a landlord is willing to spend on customizing or upgrading a rental space for a tenant. Knowing the typical TIA in your market helps you negotiate better deals for tenants.
- **Market Annual Escalation:** This is the rate at which rent increases annually. Understanding the

standard escalation rates in the market allows you to forecast future costs accurately and make informed decisions.

- **Market Amount of Free Rent Concession:** Free rent concessions are periods during which the tenant pays no rent. These are incentives to attract tenants. Knowing your market's typical free rent concessions can help you structure attractive lease agreements.
- **Availability and Vacancy in a Market:** You need to know the current supply of available rental spaces and the vacancy rates. High vacancy rates might indicate a tenant's market, where negotiation power is higher, while low vacancy rates suggest a landlord's market.
- **Absorption of Vacant Space in a Market:** Absorption rates measure the leasing rate of vacant spaces. High absorption rates indicate strong demand, while low rates suggest slower market activity. Understanding this can help anticipate market trends and make strategic decisions.

Focusing on these factual data points can help you make more informed decisions and avoid the pitfalls of flawed logic. This approach strengthens your position in negotiations and ensures that your strategies are grounded in reality, thereby reducing risks and increasing the chances of success.

Communicate Clearly

Be able to tell your clients where the subject property fits into the narrative. Knowledge is valuable when landlords are acquiring a new asset or looking to switch brokers. The team with the knowledge and facts and who can best position the asset based on concrete data will usually win the listing assignment.

Likewise, the broker/agent with the most knowledge of particular information in a specific sub-market will likely garner the tenant rep assignment. Some brokers think more information is better. I subscribe to the fact that better information is better.

> **Pro Tip: Gather and show the client what they need to know. A fatter binder or longer slide deck is not necessarily better. Focus on quality, not quantity.**

In short, you can't predict the economy or much else. You can't control outcomes, only processes that help you serve your market. With experience, it's OK to have an opinion with landlord and tenant clients, but more importantly, you should be well-versed in historical and current data.

Know your market better than your competitors. That's one way to provide exceptional value to your clients and team—the subject matter knowledge I referenced earlier in the book, along with CRE market knowledge. If you are a medical, retail, or office broker, know more than the other guy.

Data-Driven Decisions

Earlier in the book, I referenced the scenario where the landlord quoted $28 per square foot for rent. The tenant asked for $24, and the deal ended at $26.

You don't want to negotiate this way for your client, owner, or buyer. With all your data at your fingertips, subscribe to CoStar, Loopnet, and CREXI, and routinely talk with other agents to be informed in your local market.

Use the most current and reliable data to stay ahead of the competition and serve your client well. Stay informed, be disciplined, and subscribe to the sources of information that give you a competitive edge. Multimedia will provide rent information, but "old-fashioned" market knowledge allows you to figure out TIA, free rent, and other market concessions.

Regardless of which party you represent, your client relies on your knowledge, not a "salami negotiation" like the example above. Nobody wants to work with an amateur. Tenants can ask for lower rent, more TIA, and more free rent, and landlords can try to get higher rent and give up fewer concessions on their own.

Be the pro, not the amateur. I am average in golf and enjoy the game. As I do not play for a living, I don't take it that seriously and have realistic expectations of how I will play any given round. In CRE, you strive to be a professional, not an amateur. You have a state license and a fiduciary duty to your client. Research the abundant data, make informed decisions, and professionally advise your clients.

I find a lot of agents and brokers basically "fake it until they make it." Unfortunately, they do not have longevity in this business. Erroneously, many look at real estate brokerage strictly as sales. Don't become one of the agents who never learns, no matter how long they are in the business.

I challenge you to look at real estate as the career that it is. Common sense indicates that there is a reason every state requires you to have a license and maintain that license with continuing education throughout your entire career. Selling many products does not require a state license.

Chapter 8

The Power of Successful Role Models

"You are the average of the five people you spend the most time with."

—Jim Rohn

Jim Rohn was an American entrepreneur, author, and motivational speaker. Born on September 17, 1930, in Yakima, Washington, Rohn began his professional life as a stock clerk for Sears before joining a direct-selling business called AbundaVita.

Rohn passed away in December 2009, leaving a rich legacy of work, including his books, *The Five Major Pieces to the Life Puzzle* and *My Philosophy for Successful Living*.

Rohn's famous quote summarizes his belief in the power of personal associations and their influence on individual success. His teachings have inspired many successful speakers and entrepreneurs, including Tony Robbins.

I couldn't have found a better quote to open this chapter because building a booming real estate business is based mainly on your ability to learn from successful role models who inspire you to stay focused, be disciplined, and serve your clients well.

Being Coachable

If you're like me, you'll need a lot of help. It's not that smart people can't be successful on their own. It's that to be successful by learning from others means we may not have to make the same mistakes they did.

Why not learn from people who have already made many mistakes and become successful?

> **Pro Tip: You have to be willing and coachable to benefit from successful role models and mentors you can find in your office and industry.**

The fact that you're reading my book means that you're hungry to learn. You might finish my book and leave with one big idea that grabbed your attention. Who knows where you'll get inspiration and insight? What matters is you're willing to learn from others and to follow their lead. That makes you coachable.

As one example that I've already mentioned, choosing the right firm for your real estate career can make a massive difference if you're in an environment that provides what you need to be successful, including brokers and other agents who share your values, recognize you for your contributions, and provide support in the ways that empower you to be as productive as you can be every day of the working week.

Look at it the other way. If you surround yourself with negative or unmotivated people, it can hinder your growth and progress. The solution for you is to be aware of existing professional and social circles that inspire and support your vision for your real estate business.

Taking Personal Responsibility

I've been in the business for over thirty years, and I'm still learning. I see it as my responsibility to focus on continuous self-improvement. Taking personal responsibility means acknowledging that your actions, decisions, and attitudes directly affect your life outcomes. It's about owning your mistakes, learning from them, and making a conscious effort to grow.

Take control of your life and make deliberate decisions about how you live and whom you spend time with. Surround yourself with positive influences who challenge and inspire you to be better. By doing so, you align your environment with your goals, making it easier to stay motivated and focused.

Personal responsibility is crucial for achieving your personal and professional success. It involves discipline, hard work, and cultivating positive habits and relationships.

> **Pro Tip: When you hold yourself accountable, you are more likely to stay committed to your goals, face challenges head-on, and persist through setbacks.**

Moreover, taking personal responsibility builds trust and respect with others. People appreciate those who can admit their mistakes and take steps to rectify them. This quality is essential in personal and professional relationships as it fosters a culture of accountability and continuous improvement.

In essence, personal responsibility is about taking charge of your life. It empowers you to create your desired future through intentional actions and choices. By focusing on self-improvement and surrounding yourself with supportive individuals, you set the stage for lasting success and fulfillment.

Here are several of the role models who helped me the most:

Roger Staubach

> *"Confidence doesn't come out of nowhere. It's a result of something . . . hours and days and weeks and years of constant work and dedication."*
>
> *– Roger Staubach*

Roger Staubach was born on February 5, 1942. His first claim to fame is a former professional football quarterback who played for the Dallas Cowboys. Known for his leadership and athletic skills, Staubach led the Cowboys to two Super Bowl victories and earned the nickname "Captain America."

After retiring from football in 1979, Staubach ventured full-time into the real estate industry. In 1977, while still playing football, he founded The Staubach Company, a commercial real estate firm. His company revolutionized the brokerage business by focusing on tenant representation, a relatively new concept. This approach helped clients navigate complex real estate transactions, reshaping industry standards.

Staubach's impact on real estate was profound. Under his leadership, The Staubach Company grew into one of the most successful real estate firms in the US, merging with Jones Lang LaSalle in 2008. His influence extended beyond business practices; he emphasized integrity and client-focused service, earning respect and admiration in the industry.

Ted Lerner

Ted Lerner, born Theodore Nathan Lerner on October 15, 1925, was a prominent real estate developer and the managing principal owner of the Washington Nationals baseball team. Lerner's journey to becoming one of the wealthiest people in the Washington, DC, area began humbly.

After serving in the US Army during World War II and graduating from the George Washington University Law School, Lerner entered the real estate business with a $250 loan from his wife, Annette. This modest beginning laid the foundation for what would become Lerner Enterprises, one of the region's most significant private real estate development and management companies.[22]

Founded in 1952, Lerner Enterprises started by selling homes for developers. Ted Lerner's commitment to hard work and entrepreneurial spirit allowed him to expand his business into commercial real estate.

Over the decades, Lerner Enterprises grew to encompass a diverse portfolio of office buildings, shopping centers, residential properties, and hotels. Lerner's hands-on approach and dedication to quality helped him build a reputation for excellence in the real estate industry.[23]

Ted Lerner made headlines in 2006 when he purchased the Washington Nationals for $450 million. Under his ownership, the team experienced significant improvements, culminating in their first World Series championship in 2019. Lerner's involvement in the Nationals highlighted his ability to apply his business acumen to sports management, enhancing the value and success of the franchise.[24]

Reflecting on the Nationals' journey, he once said with a smile, "I might add, we're not concerned with the World Series this year," which highlights his focus on the long-term growth and development of the team rather than immediate successes.[25]

---

[22] https://en.wikipedia.org/wiki/Ted_Lerner

[23] https://lerner.com/about/

[24] https://www.forbes.com/profile/ted-lerner/

[25] https://www.washingtontimes.com/topics/ted-lerner/

Foulger-Pratt

Foulger-Pratt is a prominent real estate investment and development firm established in 1963. Sid Foulger founded the Potomac, Maryland-based company, significantly impacting my career.

In 1996, Foulger-Pratt decided to develop a medical office building. As a local firm, they wanted to hire a broker who was a medical expert. I leased a 65,000-square-foot building for them in Olney, Maryland.

I had a sense of their reputation, but the more I did business with them and got to know them better, the more I interacted with them. The leaders at Foulger-Pratt trusted me implicitly, and I leased all of that space "on a handshake" without a written listing agreement.

That was how significant our relationship had become. It's one example of how important it is to build relationships with people you like, respect, and trust. Look for local ownership and a brand that serves as a strong pillar in the community and has an excellent reputation.

Here's what that first deal led to over the following ten years:

- Leasing a new 65,000-square-foot building that they developed in Olney, Maryland.
- Leasing a 75,000-square-foot building in Landsdown, Virginia.
- Leasing a 60,000-square-foot building in Silver Spring.
- Leasing a 110,000-square-foot building in Ashburn, Virginia.

Foulger-Pratt built a reputation for long-term investment strategy and seemed knowledgeable in executing complex real estate projects. The firm's portfolio includes over fifteen million square feet of commercial, office, and multifamily residential properties across the United States.

I can't emphasize enough the power of successful role models as you build your career. Whether you're just starting your career or have decades of experience, surrounding yourself with people who exemplify excellence and integrity can profoundly impact your professional journey.

Successful role models like Roger Staubach and Ted Lerner have demonstrated that hard work, dedication, and a commitment to continuous improvement can lead to extraordinary achievements. Staubach's transition from a football legend to a real estate mogul and Lerner's rise from a modest beginning to owning a Major League Baseball team testify to the transformative power of perseverance and strategic thinking.

Being coachable and open to learning from others' experiences allows you to avoid common pitfalls and accelerate your growth. Choosing the right firm and professional circle that aligns with your values and goals can provide the support and inspiration needed to thrive.

Pro Tip: Personal responsibility is crucial in this process as it empowers you to take charge of your life and make intentional choices that drive success.

Ultimately, the relationships you build and the mentors you choose to guide you will shape your path in the real estate industry. You set the stage for a fulfilling and prosperous career by learning from the best and holding yourself accountable.

Surround yourself with those who challenge you to improve, and you'll find that their influence will help you reach new heights in your personal and professional life.

Chapter 9

Building Your Team

"Talent wins games, but teamwork and intelligence win championships."

– Michael Jordan

Michael Jordan's quote highlights a fundamental truth about success in any competitive field, especially sports. Jordan, widely regarded as one of the greatest basketball players of all time, understood that while individual talent is crucial for winning games, the sustained success of winning championships requires a cohesive team effort and strategic intelligence.

Even if you're not an athlete, you can appreciate the perspective of what it takes to win at the highest level of any sport or business. From a peer perspective, Jordan's quote emphasizes the importance of each player's role within a team.

Sure, talented individuals can deliver standout performances. Still, the synergy of the team—each player executing their specific role and supporting one another—leads to long-term success.

This principle is just as important in real estate if you intend to be successful. You don't need to play at Jordan's level. Still, you can see how the skills and contributions of his teammates, like Scottie Pippen and Dennis Rodman, complimented Jordan's extraordinary talent. Their collective effort, guided by strategic play and mutual support, was crucial for securing six NBA championships.

Coaches play a pivotal role in helping players win, and

you could say the same about brokers. Phil Jackson's coaching philosophy, which included the "triangle offense," emphasized teamwork and intelligent play. He encouraged players to work together, trust each other, and make smart decisions on the court. Jackson's ability to integrate individual skills into a well-coordinated team was instrumental in the Bulls' dominance during the 1990s.

> **Pro Tip: Plug into your firm or team's game plan and do your best. Short of that, you'll need to build your strategy and team.**

Investing in Your Team and Network

Over the last four decades, we have advanced from hiring acquaintances to utilizing a professional "headhunting" agency. We revamp our hiring methods and strategies yearly to keep up with current environmental changes.

Our philosophy of hiring young, intelligent, and hungry people has always stayed the same, but our way of finding those people evolves with the times and technology. I encourage all of my agents to keep up with the times and the ever-evolving commercial real estate business.

My team knows more about healthcare than any other medical CRE brokerage firm. Subject matter expertise is a massive component of being sharper than your competition.

The firm you work for and the team you're on make a big difference. Your current firm and any team you're a part of are essential to your network. If you're new in your career and part of a strong team with an excellent reputation in your market, it can help you feel more confident when networking and building relationships. You may not feel as vulnerable or intimidated as you would when working on your own.

Networking is about expanding your contact list and cultivating meaningful relationships with people with similar core values and goals. In other words, your network of relationships, including the team and firm you're with, is one of the most important investments you can make.

The more experience you have completing transactions, the more you learn about people. You'll meet professional people who do their jobs well because they take their careers seriously. You'll encounter others who may look great at first, but after doing business one or more times, you learn whether they pay attention to details.

Pro Tip: The top-performing professionals in every industry focus on the details because that makes complex transactions work smoothly, and people like that. People do business with people they like and trust.

You also learn how people act when a transaction or client interaction starts sideways. It's up to you to be aware of unethical behavior and stay clear if you want to build and maintain an excellent reputation.

Like many businesses, real estate is a people business. People play different roles in each transaction. Transactions that go smoothly do so because the people doing their respective jobs do them well. If not, transactions don't go well, people lose time and money, and sometimes they get sued.

I remember when we assisted our first dentist in the early nineties. The number of people involved in the transaction was overwhelming. It took me a few deals to understand that I needed to know all the team players and build a great relationship with them.

Here's a list of the people typically involved in transactions like this:

1. Dentist
2. Dental professional spouse, if applicable
3. Tenant broker
4. Landlord broker
5. Lender
6. Dental equipment vendor
7. Lawyer
8. Accountant
9. Designer
10. General contractor

Managing these many relationships requires tremendous patience. It's imperative to be part of a well-aligned team. What I mean by well-aligned is that everyone's unique abilities are in place, and deals go smoothly.

Everyone knows their role on the team, and they get their work done like true professionals. I once worked on a transaction with a dental equipment supply professional. He was excellent and brought value as an equipment rep because he knew his products well.

But one day, he drove one of my clients around to look at vacant space in shopping centers. I asked him why he did that, and he told me he wanted to "differentiate himself from his competition."

The problem was he knew nothing useful about commercial real estate because he wasn't a licensed real estate professional. He was a dental equipment supply salesman. He would not have known the answers to any of the questions my clients typically ask, such as:

- How big was the space?
- What was the asking rate?
- What was the TIA allowance?
- How much free rent was offered?
- Would the landlord lease to a dentist?

Even though I'm sure he was trying to be helpful and sincere about differentiating himself, think of the disservice he provided. He made the process much more timely and challenging.

Pro Tip: "You need to tell how the cow ate the cabbage."

In other words, there is a "right" way to facilitate a commercial real estate transaction with a licensed real estate professional. As a real estate professional, I know how to "stay in my lane."

If you ask Sherry, you never want to be "too big for your britches." That means sticking to your business and doing your best to serve your clients well by doing what you know.

Great Players Add Value

Just like Health-Pro Realty Group has a healthcare niche, other vendors do as well. All the players must know their part and how to work together. By focusing on their niche and facilitating lots of transactions, they can increase their value to future clients.

The quality of your relationships drives commercial real estate success. When people involved in your real estate transactions know their part and add lots of value, your reputation will reflect that.

In contrast, imagine a home remodeler trying to do a great job building a particular dental office. It's not going to happen. Dentists have specialized needs for their office space, and there's no way a builder without significant experience can get the job done on time and within budget.

Another common scenario we run into with dentists is that most lenders won't make loans to them. One reason for this is that most dentists graduate with significant student loan debt, making financing more difficult. That means you need to be versed in lenders that specialize in dental and will underwrite accordingly.

The cost of opening a new dental office is enormous. The dentist may need an additional $500,000-$700,000 in working capital. A non-dental lender will likely review the current debt load and decline the loan. A dental lender, understanding that dental professionals have a default rate of less than one percent, is more likely to approve the loan.

Again, the more transactions you complete, the more precise you will be on what you did well and what you could have done better. In other words, by knowing your part well, you know how to play it well because of your experience.

Pro Tip: If you lack experience, lean into the experience of your broker or team. Being part of a team enables you to leverage their momentum and plug into a business unit with crucial players, systems, and a reputation based on their track record of transactions.

We measure success in real estate in deals closed and commissions won and earned. The better you learn to play your part, the more you'll likely earn. That's how it is because the world still worships the almighty dollar for now.

If you specialize like our firm, you'll know about the nuances of your niche like we do in medical and dental transactions. For example, as brokers, we can get the dentist a landlord-tenant improvement allowance and free rent as part of most deals.

Here's another example of the importance of professionals playing their part like champs. A lawyer who works with dentists knows his clients' needs. They will advise their client if the dental equipment remains with the landlord or tenant at lease expiration. They will also understand if dental materials are considered hazardous waste. They will know many more things about a dental office transaction than a generalist.

It can be expensive to work with the wrong professionals in any field. That's why it's essential to build relationships, ask for introductions and referrals, and follow up with people in your network who can influence better transaction outcomes.

Another thing to consider is a non-dental lawyer who needs to learn dental leases or transactions may charge the tenant more to understand the intricacies of a dental deal. It's always important to consider every person involved in your transactions so that you can manage the relationships and complete a smooth transaction.

Experience matters, and having experienced people on your deals matters. The "right team" of professionals will streamline the entire process, saving time and money. Even if the team of surrounding players will change, you must remain hungry to learn, grow, and be a top-tier professional.

Shared Values

The importance of shared values in any relationship, including professional ones, cannot be overstated. In commercial real estate, where transactions are complex and stakes are high, having a team that shares common core values is crucial. These values guide decision-making, influence strategies, and determine how team members interact with each other and clients.

Shared values in a team create a foundation for trust, respect, and mutual support. When team members align their values and goals, it fosters an environment where collaboration is seamless and communication is open and honest. This alignment ensures everyone works toward the same objectives, leading to more efficient cooperation and better project outcomes.

In the high-stakes world of commercial real estate, teams that operate on a shared value system are better equipped to handle the complexities of transactions. Their unified approach enables them to navigate challenges more effectively.

Pro Tip: Competent and trustworthy team members, bound by shared values, are critical to the success of any real estate team and transaction.

Moreover, shared values extend beyond internal team dynamics to influence client relationships. Clients are likelier to trust and continue working with a team that demonstrates consistent ethical behavior and integrity. This trust can lead to long-term partnerships and repeat business, which are invaluable in commercial real estate.

Ultimately, shared values are the glue that holds these teams together. They provide a moral and ethical compass that guides actions and decisions, ensuring that all team members are competent and aligned in their commitment to excellence and integrity. In a field where the quality of relationships can make or break a deal, investing in a team with shared values is investing in the foundation of success.

Accountability and Alignment

Aligning a real estate team's goals with individual goals is critical for achieving success. Creating an aligned culture necessitates fostering an environment of honesty, support, and respect.

This alignment ensures that all team members work toward common objectives, enhancing collaboration and efficiency. Here are five fundamentals for improving your team's accountability and alignment.

1. **Setting Clear Objectives:** Clearly defined goals are the foundation of team alignment. By establishing common objectives, team members can understand their roles and how their contributions impact their success. Regularly revisiting these goals ensures everyone stays focused and motivated.
2. **Implementing Accountability Systems:** Accountability is essential for maintaining team performance. Accountability involves setting expectations, monitoring progress, and providing feedback. Tools such as biannual check-ins, weekly pipeline reports, and performance reviews help ensure that agents remain accountable and committed to their goals.
3. **Fostering Open Communication:** Effective communication is critical to successful team alignment. Open dialogue allows team members to express their ideas, concerns, and achievements, fostering a supportive and collaborative environment. This transparency builds trust and strengthens the team's cohesion.

4. **Continuous Training and Development:** Investing in ongoing training and professional development ensures team members have the latest industry knowledge and skills. Ongoing development enhances performance and demonstrates a commitment to growth, leading to higher job satisfaction and retention.

5. **Emphasizing Ethical Practices:** Upholding ethical standards is paramount in real estate. Ensuring that all team members adhere to these standards promotes integrity and builds a positive reputation for the team. This moral foundation supports long-term success and client trust.

You're part of the team at your firm level or maybe on a team within your firm. Building a booming commercial real estate business is a team and contact sport. Aligning team goals with individual objectives, establishing accountability systems, fostering open communication, providing continuous training, and emphasizing ethical practices are all crucial for achieving alignment and accountability within a real estate team.

Real estate transaction success hinges on your team's strength and cohesiveness. Michael Jordan's insight that "Talent wins games, but teamwork and intelligence win championships" underscores the importance of collective effort and strategic collaboration. Investing in your team and network is crucial; each member's role from brokers to vendors must be clearly defined and executed professionally.

Building solid relationships and aligning shared values within your team fosters trust and cooperation, which are essential for navigating complex transactions.

Pro Tip: Continuous training and high ethical standards ensure your team operates efficiently and effectively.

Accountability and alignment are vital to achieving success. Clear objectives, open communication, and regular feedback help maintain focus and motivation. By leveraging your team's collective experience and expertise, you can enhance performance and achieve sustained success in the competitive real estate market.

Chapter 10

Feitel Business Blueprint

"Strategic planning is worthless—unless there is first a strategic vision."

—John Naisbitt

Where do you see yourself in three to five years? This chapter clarifies your goals and the steps to achieve them.

You are a business owner, whether you know it or not. Unless you're Steve Jobs and don't believe having a business plan is essential, think again.

The Feitel Business Blueprint is a hybrid business plan incorporating traditional strategic and marketing plan elements. Most people in commercial real estate are motivated by making money. The best way to make more money is to be a better commercial real estate professional focused and committed to taking necessary steps to promote, market, and serve clients well.

Pro Tip: It's a business plan or blueprint you can write yourself. You can build your entire business by keeping your blueprint up-to-date.

If you see every workday as your inventory of time to invest, your business blueprint will show you and anyone on your team where to invest their time and skills working toward the shared goals.

If you're a business of one, you write the blueprint by and

for yourself. If you're part of an existing team and you don't have a marketing plan or strategic plan similar to mine, ask your broker or team leader what they think about working on a plan as a team during a few three-hour sessions.

Either way, by writing your business blueprint yourself, you're training for the big leagues because if you ask any leader of successful companies, teams, or organizations about their strategic plan, they'll be able to tell you their process and how it benefits them.

> **Pro Tip: The larger the organization, the more critical it is to have a business plan that aligns your team to the shared vision, mission, and goals.**

Understanding Your Inner Drive

While pursuing financial independence is a powerful motivator, exploring what truly drives you beyond accumulating wealth is essential. Financial independence can offer the freedom to pursue passions, spend more time with loved ones, and live on your terms, but the journey involves deeper personal motivations and self-awareness.

1. **Sense of Purpose:** Financial independence often enables people to pursue meaningful goals and projects that align with their values and passions. Knowing what excites and motivates you can provide a clear direction and enhance your commitment to your financial goals.
2. **Personal Growth:** The journey toward financial independence requires continuous learning and personal development. Embrace opportunities to

grow, acquire new skills, and expand your knowledge. This growth mindset can drive you to overcome challenges and achieve tremendous success.

3. **Autonomy and Freedom:** Many people desire autonomy—the ability to make choices without financial constraints. This freedom allows you to design a lifestyle that reflects your preferences and values, providing a sense of fulfillment and happiness.
4. **Recognition and Appreciation:** Financial independence can also be about gaining recognition and appreciation for your hard work and success. Acknowledgment by peers and loved ones can be a significant motivator, driving you to strive for excellence.

Knowing Yourself: Strengths and Weaknesses

It's crucial to have a deep understanding of your strengths and weaknesses. This self-awareness enables you to leverage your strengths effectively and address or delegate your weaknesses.

- **Self-Assessment:** Regularly evaluate your skills, competencies, and areas for improvement. Tools like SWOT analysis (Strengths, Weaknesses, Opportunities, Threats) can provide valuable insights.
- **Focus on Strengths:** Concentrate on tasks that align with your strengths to maximize efficiency and effectiveness.
- **Delegate Weaknesses:** Identify tasks that others can better handle. Delegating frees up your time

and ensures that tasks are completed by those best suited for them.

Understanding what drives you beyond financial independence and leveraging your strengths while addressing your weaknesses can create a balanced and fulfilling journey toward your goals.

Clarity of Vision

John Naisbitt's quote at the beginning of this chapter emphasizes the importance of having a clear, overarching vision before diving into the detailed strategic planning steps. If you're unsure if you need a simple business plan to help you build a booming business, think again.

Here are some benefits of having a clear vision for your business supported by a written, strategic blueprint or plan:

1. **Provides Direction:** A strategic vision outlines an organization's long-term goals and desired future state. Without this vision, planning lacks purpose and direction. It's like setting out on a journey without knowing the destination.
2. **Guides Decision-Making:** A well-defined vision helps prioritize initiatives and allocate resources effectively. It ensures that every action taken aligns with your broader goals.
3. **Motivates and Inspires:** Vision can inspire and motivate you and your team, giving them a sense of purpose and direction. When everyone understands the ultimate goal, it fosters unity and drives collective effort toward achieving it.

4. **Prevents Wasted Efforts:** Without a vision, strategic planning can lead to fragmented efforts and initiatives that may not contribute to the organization's success. A clear vision ensures that all plans and actions are purposeful and coherent.
5. **Fosters Clarity:** When you're clear about your vision and the path to get there, you'll know how to eliminate unnecessary distractions or action steps.
6. **Fosters Confidence:** The more confident you are about building a booming business, the easier it will be to take action, measure results, and find ways to improve the outcome.

Vision and Mission

Your success in commercial real estate starts with your vision and mission. If you see yourself as successful, you are on the right path. The business of life is a game of confidence, and when you're clear about what you want and how to get it, your confidence will produce measurable results.

Your vision is what you see for yourself in the future. Your ability to get where you're going depends on your ability to plan, navigate, and adapt to the unexpected.

Your mission is what you do. You are in the business of commercial real estate. You choose the market to serve and start acting to drum up business. I've already laid out how Sherry and I got started together. From our humble beginnings, we found our niche in medical and dental.

Pro Tip: Give yourself the benefit of a reasonable three- to five-year vision and set of goals.

The Essential Elements of Planning and Strategy

As you read the following core elements of your new strategic blueprint, find a notebook or create a new document to use my formula for planning your success. Again, if it's just you, finish the first draft of your plan and see how you feel. If you have a business partner or team, inviting them to create the plan with you might make sense.

Remember, you're building a business with a local or regional focus. It's your job to be an expert on your market, especially the nuances that affect the value you deliver to your clients. So keep this in mind when crafting your plan.

Write your first draft of your blueprint using what I give you. Your blueprint will evolve as you update it each month or quarter. It's up to you to keep your plan current.

The best way to use this information is to create a new document for yourself and start writing your blueprint as best you can. There's no such thing as perfect. Start writing your plan and improve it as you build a booming real estate business.

Here are the elements of effective business planning emphasizing creating revenue:

1. **Market Research and Analysis**
    - Conduct thorough research on market trends, demand, and competition.
    - Perform a SWOT (Strengths, Weaknesses, Opportunities, Threats) analysis to understand the market's strengths, weaknesses, opportunities, and threats.

- Gather data from reliable sources such as industry reports, surveys, and competitor analyses.
- Analyze the economic, social, and technological factors affecting the market.

2. **Brand Positioning**
   - Establish a strong brand identity that resonates with the target audience. Create a brand personality that reflects your core values and is relatable to your audience. Think about your tone of voice, visual style, and messaging that align with the audience's expectations and values.
   - Ensure consistent messaging and visual elements across all marketing materials. You can leverage assets your firm has already created and approved.
   - Develop a brand story highlighting your mission, values, and vision. Remember, you are a brand within your firm's brand. Be sure to remain aligned.
3. **Target Audience Identification**
   - Define the target market and buyer personas based on demographics, psychographics, and purchasing behaviors.
   - Identify the target audience's specific needs, pain points, and motivations.
   - Segment the audience into different groups to tailor marketing strategies accordingly.

4. **Value Proposition**
    - Develop a clear value proposition that addresses the specific needs and problems of the target audience.
    - Create a concise statement communicating your product or service's unique benefits and value.
    - Ensure the value proposition differentiates your offering from competitors'.
5. **Marketing Channels**
    - Identify and select the most effective marketing channels to reach the target audience.
    - Utilize online advertising, social media, email marketing, direct mail, and other relevant channels.
    - Develop a multi-channel strategy to maximize reach and engagement.
6. **Content Creation**
    - Create engaging and relevant content tailored to the target audience.
    - Develop a content calendar to plan and schedule blogs, videos, whitepapers, and other content formats.
    - Focus on providing value through informative, educational, and entertaining content.
7. **Lead Generation Strategy**
    - Implement strategies to attract and capture leads, such as offering free resources, hosting webinars, and running promotions.

- Utilize lead magnets like eBooks, checklists, and free trials to entice potential customers.
- Develop landing pages optimized for conversions.

8. **Sales Funnel Development**
    - Design a sales funnel that guides leads through the buyer journey from awareness to decision.
    - Create stages for awareness, consideration, and decision, with specific content and actions for each stage.
    - Use marketing automation tools to nurture leads through the funnel.
9. **Partnerships and Networking**
    - Build relationships with industry partners, influencers, and thought leaders.
    - Attend networking events, trade shows, and conferences to expand your reach and build credibility.
    - Collaborate with partners on joint marketing initiatives.
10. **Budget Allocation**
    - Determine the budget for each marketing activity based on expected ROI.
    - Allocate resources to the most effective channels and strategies.
    - Monitor spending and adjust the budget as needed to optimize results.

11. **Performance Metrics**
    - Set measurable goals and key performance indicators (KPIs) to track the marketing plan's effectiveness.
    - Use metrics like website traffic, conversion rates, lead generation, and sales performance.
    - Regularly review performance data and adjust strategies accordingly.
12. **Execution Timeline**
    - Create a detailed timeline for the implementation of each marketing activity.
    - Assign responsibilities and deadlines to team members.
    - Use project management tools to track progress and ensure timely execution.
13. **Review and Optimization**
    - Regularly review performance data to assess the success of marketing activities.
    - Identify areas for improvement and optimize strategies based on results.
    - Conduct A/B testing to refine tactics and enhance effectiveness.

Plan to Succeed

Remember, strategic planning without a strategic vision is worthless. Knowing where you want to be in three to five years is crucial. This chapter has helped you clarify your goals and the steps to achieve them.

You are a business owner, whether you recognize it or not. Even if you're not Steve Jobs, having a business plan is essential. The Feitel Business Blueprint combines traditional strategic and marketing elements to help you succeed in commercial real estate.

Writing your business blueprint keeps your goals and actions aligned. If you're a solo professional, create the plan yourself. If you're part of a team, work together on it. This blueprint trains you for the big leagues, ensuring every step aligns with your strategic vision.

Understanding your inner drive and leveraging your strengths while addressing weaknesses is vital. A clear vision provides direction, guides decision-making, and motivates you and your team. It prevents wasted efforts and fosters confidence.

Your success in commercial real estate starts with your vision and mission. Your vision is your future goal, and your mission is what you do to serve others. Stay committed to your strategic blueprint, keep it updated, and let it guide your journey toward achieving your goals.

By focusing on planning, strategy, and understanding your motivations, you'll be well on your way to building a successful business. Remember, the larger the organization, the more critical it is to have a business plan that aligns your team with the shared vision, mission, and goals.

Stay clear, stay focused, and keep moving forward. Your strategic vision is your road map to success.

Chapter 11

Managing Your Business for Life

"The only way to do great work is to love what you do."

– Steve Jobs

The best way to build a booming commercial real estate business is to love it and do your best to become a top-producing professional. Of course, to do that, you've got to know what action steps to take at the appropriate time.

Steve Jobs's quote highlights the importance of passion and dedication in achieving excellence. Jobs believed true satisfaction and success in one's career come from loving what you do. So can you.

Pro Tip: This love for your work drives you to put in the extra effort, be creative, and strive for greatness.

You've done a great job getting this far, and now it's time to delve deeper into how to sustain and grow your business for life.

It's time to take action. Based on what you've read so far, including how to write a solid strategic blueprint, here's a recap of the suggested action steps to take:

Passion and Dedication: The Foundation of Success

Steve Jobs's wisdom reminds us that passion is not just a luxury but a necessity in the business world. When you love what you do, work ceases to be a chore and transforms into a source of joy and fulfillment. This intrinsic motivation is crucial for long-term success. Passion fuels perseverance, enabling you to overcome challenges and setbacks with resilience and determination.

Action Steps:

1. **Identify Your Passion:** Reflect on what aspects of your business you are most passionate about. Is it the thrill of closing a deal, the creativity of marketing, or the satisfaction of helping clients achieve their goals?
2. **Align Your Business Goals:** Ensure your business goals align with your passions. This alignment will keep you motivated and focused on what truly matters.
3. **Cultivate a Positive Mindset:** Surround yourself with positive influences and continuously seek inspiration. Attend industry conferences, read books, and engage with mentors who share your passion and enthusiasm.

Building a Sustainable Business Model

A sustainable business model is the backbone of long-term success. It ensures your business can adapt to changes, withstand economic fluctuations, and grow. Sustainability involves strategic planning, efficient operations, and focusing on long-term goals rather than short-term gains.

Action Steps:

1. **Develop a Clear Vision:** Define your long-term vision and mission. This clarity will guide your decisions and help you focus on your ultimate goals.
2. **Implement Efficient Processes:** Streamline your operations to maximize efficiency. Use technology to automate routine tasks, reduce waste, and improve productivity.
3. **Plan for the Future**: Create a strategic plan that includes short-term and long-term goals. Regularly review and adjust your plan to reflect changes in the market and business environment.

Financial Management: The Lifeblood of Your Business

Effective financial management is crucial for your business's sustainability and growth. It involves budgeting, forecasting, managing cash flow, and making informed financial decisions. Sound financial management practices ensure that your business remains solvent and can invest in growth opportunities.

Action Steps:

1. **Create a Budget:** Develop a comprehensive budget that outlines your expected income and expenses. Review your budget regularly and adjust it as necessary.

2. **Monitor Cash Flow:** Monitor your cash flow closely to ensure that you have enough liquidity to cover your expenses. Use cash flow management tools to track and forecast your cash flow.
3. **Invest Wisely:** Make informed investment decisions based on thorough research and analysis. Diversify your investments to minimize risk and maximize returns.

Building a Strong Team

Your team is one of your most valuable assets. A strong, cohesive team can drive your business to new heights. Building a great team involves hiring the right people, fostering a positive work culture, and providing opportunities for growth and development.

Action Steps:

1. **Hire for Fit:** Look for candidates who have the necessary skills and experience, fit well with your company culture, and share your values.
2. **Foster a Positive Culture:** Create a work environment that promotes collaboration, innovation, and respect. Recognize and reward your team's contributions.
3. **Invest in Development:** Provide ongoing training and development opportunities for your team. Encourage continuous learning and support their professional growth.

Customer Relationships: The Heart of Your Business

Strong relationships with your customers are vital for long-term success. Satisfied customers are more likely to return, refer others, and provide valuable feedback. Building and maintaining these relationships requires excellent customer service, effective communication, and a deep understanding of your customers' needs.

Action Steps:

1. **Deliver Exceptional Service:** Consistently provide high-quality products and services. Go the extra mile to exceed your customers' expectations.
2. **Communicate Effectively:** Maintain open lines of communication with your customers. Listen to their feedback and address their concerns promptly.
3. **Understand Their Needs:** Use customer data and insights to understand their preferences and behaviors. Tailor your offerings to meet their needs and build long-term loyalty.

Innovation and Adaptability: Staying Ahead of the Curve

Innovation and adaptability are crucial to staying competitive in a rapidly changing business environment. Embrace new technologies, stay abreast of industry trends, and be willing to pivot when necessary. Innovation can drive growth, improve efficiency, and provide a competitive edge.

Action Steps:

1. **Embrace Technology:** Invest in new technologies to improve operations, enhance customer experience, and drive growth.
2. **Stay Informed:** Stay current with industry trends and best practices by attending conferences, reading industry publications, and networking with other professionals.
3. **Be Willing to Pivot:** Be open to change and adapt your business model. Flexibility and responsiveness are crucial for long-term success.

Personal Development: Investing in Yourself

As a business owner, your personal growth is just as significant as your business growth. Continuously investing in your skills, knowledge, and well-being will enable you to lead your business more effectively and inspire your team.

Action Steps:

1. **Continue Learning:** Pursue ongoing education and professional development opportunities. Take courses, attend workshops, and seek mentorship.
2. **Practice Self-Care:** Prioritize your physical and mental well-being. Maintain a healthy work-life balance and engage in activities that rejuvenate you.
3. **Set Personal Goals:** Define personal goals that align with your professional aspirations. Review and adjust these goals regularly to stay on track.

Networking: Expanding Your Horizons

Networking is an essential part of managing your business. Building a solid network of industry contacts, mentors, and peers can provide support, advice, and opportunities for collaboration. Effective networking can open doors to new partnerships, clients, and markets.

Action Steps:

1. **Attend Events:** Participate in industry conferences, trade shows, and networking events. Engage with other professionals and build meaningful connections.
2. **Join Professional Associations:** Become a member of relevant industry associations and organizations. Take advantage of their resources and networking opportunities.
3. **Leverage Social Media:** Use social media platforms to connect with industry leaders, share insights, and stay informed about industry trends.

Strategic Planning: Charting Your Course

Strategic planning is critical for long-term success. It involves setting clear goals, developing a road map, and regularly reviewing your progress. Strategic planning ensures that your business stays on track and can adapt to changes in the market.

Action Steps:

1. **Set Clear Goals**: Define specific, measurable, achievable, relevant, and time-bound (SMART) goals. These goals will guide your strategic planning process.

2. **Develop a Road Map:** Create a detailed plan outlining the steps needed to achieve your goals. Assign responsibilities and set deadlines for each task.
3. **Review and Adjust:** Review your progress regularly and adjust your plan as needed. Be flexible and willing to pivot in response to market or business environment changes.

The Journey of Lifelong Success

Managing your business for life is a journey that requires passion, dedication, and continuous improvement. By focusing on these critical areas—passion and commitment, sustainability, financial management, team building, customer relationships, innovation, personal development, networking, and strategic planning—you can build a business that survives and thrives.

Remember, the only way to do great work is to love what you do. Let your passion drive you and your dedication guide you. With these principles, you can achieve lasting success and create a business that stands the test of time.

We've covered a lot of ground since the start. Let's recap what you've learned and bring this book to a close in the next and final chapter.

Chapter 12

Prospering in the Business of Life

"My strength lies solely in my tenacity."

– Louis Pasteur

You did it. By finishing this book, you're way ahead of the pack. Congratulations. Here's a quick recap of the ground we've covered.

In Chapter 1, we began our journey by discussing the basics. The chapter focused on the significant first steps, like earning a substantial commission, choosing the right firm, and setting realistic expectations. It set the stage for understanding CRE's high potential and initial challenges.

In the second chapter, we explored the foundational elements of CRE. These elements included the importance of a solid business approach, passion, and mindset. We covered the types of commercial properties, key terminology, and the crucial role of fiduciary duty, emphasizing how these fundamentals shape a successful career in real estate.

In Chapter 3, we delved into the practical aspects of CRE. We discussed mastering the fundamentals, maintaining professionalism, and understanding essential concepts. The chapter highlighted the high cost of ignorance, the importance of continuous learning, and creativity in exploring alternative property uses. It also covered niche specialization, long-term planning, and managing business risks.

Chapter 4 focused on personal branding and marketing strategies. Topics included positioning oneself professionally, building a strong brand, and the importance of core values. We also discussed key platforms, tools, community connections, and maintaining ethics and integrity in personal branding.

Chapter 5 emphasized the art of building and managing relationships, the importance of follow-ups, and effective negotiation strategies. We explored the Feitel Sales Process, the ethical considerations in sales, and techniques for closing deals successfully.

Chapter 6 shifted to brokerage services, covering tenant representation, the lease process, and the role of a tenant rep. The chapter also discussed negotiation beyond the lease, long-term relationships, property brokering, and the value of a broker. It included case studies and highlighted creative solutions and industry pioneers like Roger Staubach.

In Chapter 7, we learned that market analysis is critical in CRE and covered its components, shared resources, and suggested practical applications. We also addressed flawed logic, clear communication, and making data-driven decisions to avoid common pitfalls.

Chapter 8 focused on the impact of role models in CRE, highlighting the importance of being coachable and taking personal responsibility. We discussed influential figures like Roger Staubach, Ted Lerner, and the Foulger-Pratt company, illustrating how their successes can inspire and guide us.

Chapter 9 covered building a solid team and network. We discussed investing in your team, adding value through great players, and the importance of shared values, accountability, and alignment within a team to achieve collective success.

In Chapter 10, we worked through the Feitel Business Blueprint. I advise everyone who reads this book to write, edit, and update their blueprint at least once a quarter. It's incredible how powerful a simple, clear strategic action plan can be for building a booming business.

Chapter 11 was about learning to manage your real estate business in ways that complement the life you want. We discussed the importance of being passionate about your work. It's much easier to stay dedicated when building your business. I reiterated how I feel about great teamwork, and I hope you'll be consistent in applying the knowledge I've gained over the years.

The Harsh Reality

I have no regrets about delivering pizza and blowing off my career as a trial lawyer now that I've built a booming business in commercial real estate. I've had a lot of help along the way, and I'm incredibly grateful for Sherry and our entire team.

If it were easy to build a booming business in any industry, more people would. But the truth is, most people can't or won't build a business they can call their own. That's just the way it is. It's a harsh reality.

The most challenging barrier to entry beyond the skills to succeed is having too much overhead or lifestyle expenses to afford to build a booming commercial real estate business. When I started, fresh out of law school, broke, I was disillusioned enough to start in a new industry—I even had to deliver pizza and do inglorious work to get what I wanted out of life.

> **Pro Tip: Let me remind you what it takes to build a booming real estate business: guts, drive, dedication, honesty, luck, and a vision you can stick with for decades.**

As if that's not enough, here are a few statistics that prove how hard it is to be a top producer in commercial real estate.

- According to Salary.com, the median real estate agent in America makes $46,461 as of the time of this writing.[26]
- There are approximately 52,310 real estate brokers in the US, including both commercial and residential brokers.[27]
- The National Association of Realtors reports that eighty-seven percent of real estate agents fail during their first five years.[28]

The fundamentals of being a top-producing residential real estate agent are similar to those for commercial real estate. One of the main differences is the average size of your transactions. In time, you will find your sweet spot. Typically, commercial real estate agents work on more significant transactions than most residential real estate agents. And the volume of transactions might be lower for commercial agents.

You will know how good you are after your first few years in the business. All businesses take time to build. If commercial real estate is your passion like it is for me and Sherry, and you stick with it using what I've shared from my direct experience, you will dramatically improve the likelihood of your success.

But it's all up to you. If you are committed to building a booming business that synchronizes with your ideal lifestyle, see everything you do as a way to live in service to your family and community. There has never been a more critical time to focus on core family values and being a great family and community member.

---

[26] https://www.salary.com/tools/salary-calculator/real-estate-agent

[27] https://www.vts.com/blog/cre-broker-value

[28] https://www.nar.realtor/research-and-statistics/quick-real-estate-statistics

Real estate is an excellent business for life, but you need a plan. Over time, it is OK to adapt the plan, but with a simple outline, the overall process will be much easier. There are no shortcuts to hard work and dedication to make this a profession. Building successful long-term client relationships takes time and sincere effort.

Consider something else if you don't truly have a passion for commercial real estate. You must understand the concept of "fiduciary duty." It is a legal concept and must be adhered to for long-term success. Have a niche, never give up, and always serve your client to the best of your ability.

Building a Business for Life

Real estate is not a job. Forget hours, hourly compensation, or a rigid schedule. You need to think about it, breathe it, and live it always. I'm not saying you must sacrifice your entire life for your business, but your business success empowers you to afford your chosen lifestyle. Always move forward and consistently put your client's interests ahead of your own.

Creativity separates amateurs from professionals. Do not be afraid to zigzag from the status quo. Design your ideal life, and you can create a legacy. Real estate allows you to build long-term wealth and, more importantly, equity. Equity refers to the ownership interest in a company. The value would return to a company's shareholders if somebody sold all the assets and paid the debts.

Equity represents the value of a business owner's investment after subtracting the company's debts or liabilities. Equity can include investments made by the owner or proceeds reinvested into the business to help it grow. Essentially, equity is what the owner truly "owns" in the business, financially speaking.

Real estate accounts for some of the largest fortunes in the world. In one of my favorite television series, *The Sopranos*, Tony says to AJ, "Buy real estate, AJ, because God isn't going to make any more of it." That's sage advice from one of the world's most famous TV mobsters.

Markets will ebb and flow, but you can build real, tangible wealth in the long term. It's not as liquid as cash, but allows freedom in your wealth-building plan. Once you own it, you will have many options for using it. It's OK if you want to make a lot of money earning real estate commissions and invest in alternative models, but real estate is hard to beat for many reasons. Owning, selling, financing, and pledging real estate creates wealth when done well and with discipline.

Game of Confidence

Business success is like everything else. It's a game of confidence, discipline, and focus on serving your clients well. The most significant benefit of having a written strategic blueprint is you will have clarity about where you're going and how to get there. When you have clarity, you have confidence.

That's why I want you to commit to writing your initial business strategic blueprint, securing your top mentor, and jumping into the deep end. Like I've said before, and I will remind you again, never fear failure if I manage or coach you.

Pro Tip: You can't fail if you see your failures as improvement opportunities. Be fearless!

Remember, I delivered pizzas and fed my family dinner three nights a week because I was that hungry and committed to building a booming business.

If you fall, pick yourself up and keep going forward always. Even the most successful real estate developers have lost buildings to the bank, and many have filed for bankruptcy once or twice. But the best of them keep bouncing back.

One of my best mentors taught me, "If you don't make mistakes, you are not learning." Conceptually, I agree with that, but with two caveats. Have a mentor to learn from, and make sure you learn from your mistakes.

While you need confidence, remember you are sometimes wrong. Listen to people who know better. I once worked on a deal with one of the wealthiest real estate owners in the Washington metropolitan area. His net worth was north of ten billion dollars.

I had made a little bit of money and was getting cocky in my own right. I was representing a "start-up" radiologist. The owner inserted a clause in the lease that my client could not open another competing location for five years. He reasoned that he wanted my client to succeed and be able to pay their rent.

Zealously representing my client, the request was demanding and a restraint of trade. I picked up the phone and, fortunately, got a voicemail. I would tell the billionaire off and puff my chest on the matter.

Fortunately, I was working from home that day, and Sherry heard the tone of my voicemail. I proudly told her what I was planning to do. She appropriately told me not to do that under any circumstance.

Sherry has always been wiser than me regarding the ways of the world. She told me this individual could put me out of business with a few phone calls and encouraged me to find a more harmonious solution. Once again, it was great advice, and to this day, I enjoy a stellar relationship with this family.

Thank you, Sherry!

Strategy and Tactics

> *"Strategy without tactics is the slowest route to victory. Tactics without strategy is the noise before defeat."*
>
> *– Sun Tzu*

Sun Tzu was a legendary figure in ancient China, renowned for his expertise in military strategy and philosophy. He lived during the Eastern Zhou period, roughly around 500 BCE. You can learn the difference between effective strategy and tactics.

You can learn a lot from wiser people and those with worldly experience. Sun Tzu is most famous for authoring *The Art of War*, a comprehensive work on military tactics and strategy that has transcended its original purpose to influence various fields beyond warfare, including business and leadership.

His teachings emphasize the importance of intelligence, strategy, and adaptability in conflict, which remain relevant today.

Have a plan and stick to it. Quantify your goals and check on them often. At least every quarter, ensure you are on track to achieving your goals. The primary focus of my book is to help you write and update a business blueprint for your success.

You can't control outcomes—nobody can. What you can control is your process for planning and getting your work done every day. Building a booming real estate business is a contact and team sport.

Never Quit

Never, ever throw in the towel once you commit. After your first blueprint draft, work closely with your mentor and teammates to communicate clearly and frequently. Building a business is a team and contact sport. Given a solid strategic blueprint fueling your focus, you will face many challenges, but always keep going.

Failures are a part of success. Always be creative and move forward. Have a plan and stick to it, but adapt and change when warranted. For example, I started the business primarily by doing landlord agency work. I was comfortable with that and enjoyed it. Midway through building the business, we took on more tenant rep work, specifically dental and eye care. We have had roughly 50-50 landlord and tenant representation work for the last five years.

Currently, I am comfortable with this blend. An equal amount of work with both landlords and tenants keeps us sharp. With firsthand experience, we know what owners and tenants seek in the market. Overall, it keeps my team sharper than the competitive shops. However, this current scenario is not "in stone."

Market conditions could easily cause us to adapt and change our mantra. Residential real estate took a dramatic turn in March 2024. The National Association of REALTORS® (NAR) settled a lawsuit that will significantly change real estate commissions.

As of July 2024, real estate sellers are no longer legally required to pay the commissions of buyers' agents. This agreement aims to increase price competition among buyers' agents and alters the traditional model where the seller pays the commissions for both the selling and buying agents.

The NAR has agreed to pay $418 million in damages as part of the settlement. This change will likely impact how agents are compensated and could lead to more direct negotiation on commission rates between buyers and their agents.

Millions of agents have made a living helping buyers for decades. Poof. In one lawsuit, everything will change.

- Will buyers be willing to pay their agent?
- Will the public be adequately protected?
- Will all of those buyer brokers stay in the real estate business?

Time will tell. Remember, you can't account for all change, but be nimble and "roll with it." Agents who adapt to this change will survive, while those who do not are in trouble.

What's Next

As I love building and putting deals together, one of my dreams is to be a real estate developer. Owning medical office space is the next logical progression for Health-Pro Realty Group and me regarding future growth and vision. Doctors, dentists, optometrists, and veterinarians rarely move from their space.

Infrastructure costs are very high, as is moving medical and dental equipment. For this reason, they typically stay in the same space for many years. Many healthcare professionals want to own their space and build equity. With thousands of clients, I know a lot of doctors and dentists. They often take what is considered a small space in commercial real estate, which is typically condos.

Unfortunately, condos do not appreciate as much as free-standing office buildings. In fact, in Rockville, Maryland, a small suburb outside of Washington, DC, medical office condos are worth less than they originally sold for in 2006. That's a terrible investment in retrospect.

Therefore, our expansion creates opportunities for doctors to own part of the real estate. We will form a partnership in which the doctors will own the building and benefit from equity appreciation as well as the other upsides of owning commercial real estate. That's the next wave of innovation for our firm.

Closing Thoughts

Here's one final anecdote from a deal we're working on: It's a $12 million sale, and the commission is $360,000. It has been up and down since January of this year. It's still not closed but is moving in the right direction.

I was at an impasse because the buyer and seller were too far apart on the due diligence period and the amount and funding of the deposit. The owner wants thirty days, and our client needs forty-five days. The deposit is from overseas, and the bank needs up to fifteen days to complete the wire transfer. The seller wants the money wired the day the contract is executed.

Once again, Sherry saved the day. We work together, and I always enlist her pearls of wisdom. She proposed the buyer post a portion of the deposit at contract execution and wire the remainder as soon as practicable. At book writing, I think we may have a "meeting of the minds."

I hope you have a teammate, spouse, or other trusted partner who can impart timely pearls of wisdom. It's a tough business, and having a trustworthy partner helps, especially when things get tough.

Our daughter often says creativity and innovation are the main differences between average and successful agents. Deals are all different. By definition, a broker has to deal with two parties with different goals and objectives. Finding a middle ground between the two parties is the difference between making or not making the deal.

If it were easy, anyone could do it. Find the middle ground, compromise, and make the deal. The more deals you close, the more money you make. Think outside the box. Adapt and change, zig and zag.

And now, here we are, ready to part ways. I wish you the best of luck as you put in the hard work to become a successful commercial real estate professional.

About Atmosphere Press

Founded in 2015, Atmosphere Press was built on the principles of Honesty, Transparency, Professionalism, Kindness, and Making Your Book Awesome. As an ethical and author-friendly hybrid press, we stay true to that founding mission today.

If you're a reader, enter our giveaway for a free book here:

SCAN TO ENTER
BOOK GIVEAWAY

If you're a writer, submit your manuscript for consideration here:

SCAN TO SUBMIT
MANUSCRIPT

And always feel free to visit Atmosphere Press and our authors online at atmospherepress.com. See you there soon!

About the Author

Charles "Chuck" Feitel, a native of Rockville, Maryland, credits his upbringing in a tight-knit community with strong family values as the bedrock of his character. Raised in a close-knit, small family where success was not just encouraged but expected, Chuck's early life was marked by significant achievements in academics and athletics, including making the basketball and track teams and taking leadership roles in student government. He also had a solid commitment to his faith. These early experiences, underpinned by the entrepreneurial spirit of his father and grandfather, shaped his values and aspirations.

Despite facing the significant obstacle of failing the bar exam, Chuck used this setback as a catalyst to reexamine and ultimately redefine his career goals. This resilience led to his proudest achievement: starting his own company and fostering a loving family. Charles believes in the power of perseverance, loyalty, and respect for those he loves and admires, values instilled in him from a young age.

Fortunately, in his late twenties, he met the love of his life, Sherry, who has proven to be a "rock" in the success of the business and family. Always offering encouragement and carrying a positive outlook, she has shaped Charles's life in many ways.

His core values of hard work, family care, and integrity have been the guiding principles of his life. Charles lives by the motto "Never give up, always be moving forward, always be learning," which shows in his daily regimen of exercise, work, and continuous self-improvement.

If Chuck were to write a memoir, it would be titled *Never Give Up: Realizing Your Goals and Dreams*, encapsulating his journey of overcoming fears and failures through perseverance. Chuck's legacy will be as a successful businessman who deeply loved and cared for his family, embodying the lessons of never giving up, loyalty, and respect.

Chuck Feitel's story is a testament to the power of resilience, the importance of family, and the unyielding pursuit of success. It offers valuable lessons for anyone looking to navigate the complexities of life and career.

Lastly, feel free to connect with Chuck on LinkedIn and send him a question or comment.

www.ingramcontent.com/pod-product-compliance
Lightning Source LLC
LaVergne TN
LVHW102010210926
848483LV00015B/450/J
9798891326484